FUSE IT
and Be Done!

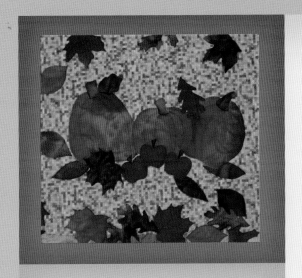

FUSIBLE WEB · FUSIBLE INTERFACING

FUSIBLE STABILIZER · BONDING AGENTS

FUSIBLE GRIDS, FLEECE & BIAS TAPE

FUSIBLE CRYSTALS, RIBBONS & THREADS

Barbara Campbell & Yolanda Fundora

©2008 Barbara Campbell and Yolanda Fundora

Published by

700 East State Street • Iola, WI 54990-0001
715-445-2214 • 888-457-2873
www.krausebooks.com

Our toll-free number to place an order or obtain
a free catalog is (800) 258-0929.

Library of Congress Cataloging-in-Publication Data
Campbell, Barbara, 1946-
    Fuse it and be done : finish projects faster using fusible products / Barbara Campbell and Yolanda Fundora. -- 1st ed.
    p. cm.
    ISBN-13: 978-0-89689-579-9 (pbk. : alk. paper)
    ISBN-10: 0-89689-579-3 (pbk. : alk. paper)
    1. Patchwork--Patterns. 2. Quilting--Patterns. 3. Fusible materials in sewing. I. Fundora, Yolanda V. II. Title.
    TT835.C3562 2008
    746.46'041--dc22

                                    2008030477

Cover Design by Michelle Thompson
Designed by Heidi Bittner-Zastrow
Edited by Stefanie Laufersweiler and Toni Toomey

Printed in China

About the Authors

Barbara Campbell

Yolanda Fundora

Having met as members of the same quilt guild just two years ago, the authors found their skills to be very complementary, as one is a passionate quilt and pattern designer with a background in marketing, and the other is a textile designer with a parallel career in fine art and illustration.

Barbara Campbell spent most of her adult working life as an executive assistant in several different industries, but always in the marketing area. She acquired important writing, merchandising and public relations skills. Once she discovered the wonderful world of quilting, she abandoned her "real job" in the corporate world to venture into her own business designing quilts and patterns. She spent some time as a technical reader for a quilting publication and then as an editor for two quilting magazines, acquiring additional skills to incorporate into her business plan. The only thing missing was the ideal partner, which she found in Yolanda.

Yolanda Fundora has been painting, drawing and designing all her life. Somewhat to her surprise, she has managed to make her present life a wonderful mixture of all the artistic activities that interest her: textile design, illustrating children's books, all kinds of fine art of the digital and not-so-digital variety, gardening and designing books and covers for a Spanish–English bilingual publisher. She is supremely lucky to share her life and home with a very talented art quilter and to have wonderful "art" discussions as daily fare. She also thanks the universe for having found Barbara at the right moment in life, a business partner of singular inventiveness and generosity of spirit.

Combining their broad-based experience, Barbara and Yolanda are now bringing fabric lines to market under the Jersey Girls brand. Almost all the fabrics used throughout the book are designed by Yolanda and printed by various manufacturers.

Visit Barbara and Yolanda's website at www.loveinstitches.com to learn more about this creative partnership.

Acknowledgments

This book has been made possible by the generosity and support of many of the companies in the industry who manufacture fusible products. We thank them for the information and products provided for us to test and use in creating our samples. The ones included in this book have been extensively tested, and we feel comfortable in recommending them to our readers.

We both want to thank our partners, families and friends for their continued support of our efforts to get the book finished. They have sometimes taken the burden of other tasks so that we could focus on the deadlines. Very special thanks and hugs to Gary and Pamela.

We also want to thank our friends in the quilt and art world who so graciously offered to share their fused pieces that appear in the book. Thank you to our contributors who spent time making projects: Nina Kolpin and Marta McDowell. (See page 127 for more on these talented ladies.)

SECTION ONE
Fusing Technique Projects...... 14

*Learn the basics of fusing with
a variety of products while making
these beautiful creations.*

Section Two
More Fusing Fun

Explore fusibles further

with these additional projects.

Introduction

Those of us who quilt, scrapbook, sew or create art and crafts in general typically have no trouble amassing mountains of fabric, paper, paints and other means to inspire us and ease us along. But one precious resource many of us have trouble getting our hands on is time. If only we had more of it, "that project" would finally be done and we'd be on to the next one.

Fusing will not only make your projects come to fruition faster, but also in a much smoother fashion. Fusing lets you easily adhere all kinds of material to just about any object or fabric, with the help of pressure and heat. It can make even the most complex project, such as an intricately designed quilt, much simpler to produce. It can hold items in place to make stitching a snap, at times even unnecessary; it can offer reinforcement when and where you need it; it can provide the solution when you're not sure of the best way to affix one thing to another. Fusing can save the day, and sometimes your sanity. Whatever your specialty, it can give the much-needed assist that propels your projects toward completion.

For this book, we fused in every way, on anything we could think of, with all the fusible products and embellishments we could get our hands on. Still, we have only scratched the surface of what can be done with them. By doing the projects within these pages, you will learn how to use a variety of fusible products readily available in craft, quilt and art supply shops. We hope you'll pick up many new and exciting creative ideas to try along the way. The following pages give you a basic introduction to fusibles and the tools you need for fusing, then it's on to the projects. The templates and patterns necessary for all the projects are supplied on the CD that came with the book. Welcome to the wonderful world of fusing!

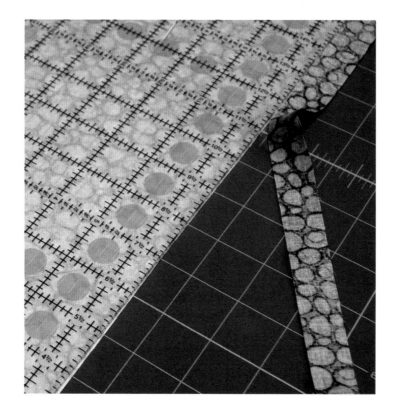

Basic Fusible Products

Many of these products are interchangeable, depending on what you find locally and what materials you are fusing with them. Do some tests on scrap material to learn the unique characteristics and advantages of each product, and to decide which one best suits each individual project. In the projects in this book, we are specific about the products used when they gave us good results, but that shouldn't stop you from researching and trying other possibilities.

Fusible Web

Fusible web is an iron-on-adhesive that bonds two layers of material. When you apply a hot iron to the material on top, the heat fuses it to the bottom material by melting the layer of fusible web in between.

Some fusible web products come with pressure-sensitive adhesive on one side, providing a temporary bond to the appliqué material until you are ready to fuse. Others have it on both sides, which allows you to also create a temporary bond to both the appliqué material and the receiving material. This makes it easy to reposition the appliqué as needed before making its placement permanent.

There are several popular brands of fusible web on the market. Two of the most readily available are Steam-A-Seam® and Steam-A-Seam 2® by The Warm™ Company and Wonder-Under® by Pellon®. Others available include Floriani's Appli-Kay Wonder and Therm O Web's HeatnBond®.

Most fusible web comes with paper backing (also called release paper), making it easier to handle and for tracing on any shapes or designs to be cut out of the appliqué material to be fused. It is usually sold by the yard on bolts or rolls; Steam-A-Seam products also conveniently come in ¼" and ½" tapes.

For several projects we used Steam-A-Seam. Besides fabric-only projects, Steam-A-Seam products are well suited for dimensional pieces and crafting on wood and metal, as well as multi-surface items such as mixed-media collages and paper art.

We used Steam-A-Seam 2, a double-stick, fusible adhesive, to cover a wooden tissue box with fabric.

Among your considerations when choosing a fusible web is the drape you want any fabric projects to have. Steam-A-Seam and the heavier nonwoven fusible webs add more body to a work and are more appropriate for wall hangings, art quilts, table runners and place mats. Anything requiring a soft drape should use lightweight or woven fusibles, such as Mistyfuse™. This very lightweight, sheer fusible web creates a long-lasting bond without adding extra bulk. It is also environmentally friendly (solvent-free and recyclable). However, it does not come with a paper backing. We used it to create fusible batting on some of the smaller quilting projects, to attach some sheer fabrics such as tulle and chiffon to backgrounds and as a shading element on an art quilt.

Wonder-Under is another possibility for quilts and wearables where a soft drape is desired. Temporary spray adhesives and bonding powders provide another option when you need a lightweight bond, which we'll discuss later.

Fusible Interfacing/Stabilizer

Available in either woven or non-woven styles—in several brands and various forms—fusible interfacings or stabilizers give added support or reinforcement, and are particularly useful for machine embroidery. Cut-away or tear-away stabilizers offer temporary support and prevent unwanted shifting while you are working with delicate, flimsy, stretchy or otherwise unstable fabric. They are fused to the back of the fabrics to stabilize them while embroidering, then removed. Floriani's water-soluble fusible stabilizer is removed by soaking in water to return the pliability of the fabric. We used this to stabilize some of our fused appliqué for the machine-stitching on the edges and found it to work well.

You'll find various weights and varieties of stiffness of the non-woven interfacing. We have found it both with and without fusible. The woven interfacing is a more pliable product where a soft interfacing touch is needed. Some are available in both black and white, to suit every need. Floriani's No Show Nylon Mesh Fusible is translucent and invisible to the eye when viewed from the front of the piece.

Fusible Batting

When machine quilting, fusible batting provides a quick and easy way to baste (or temporarily hold together) the quilt layers in preparation for the quilting process. The layers will not shift as you do your stitching, and you are spared the hassle of pinning.

There are several fusible batting products you can try, including June Tailor® Quilter's Fusible Batting™, which can remain in the quilt if you want more body, or be rinsed away. You can also make your own fusible batting by combining regular cotton or cotton-blend batting with Mistyfuse, bonding powder or temporary spray adhesive.

Fusible Fleece

We tried several brands of fusible fleece, including Floriani's Heat N Sta Fusible Light Fleece®, for some of the book's projects. These products have fusing on one side, which helps the fibers stay put while stitching. They are useful for giving soft but less-bulky padding than batting to items such as place mats. Always lay your fabric on top of the glue side of the fleece to press.

Firm Fusible Stabilizer

There are several brands of firm fusible stabilizer, which come in two versions, with glue on one or both sides. They offer stiff, sturdy, perma-

nent support that's useful for dimensional projects. Floriani's double-sided, fusible Stitch N Shape® is one option. The popular stabilizer Timtex™ doesn't have the fusible built in, but it can be used with fusible web, such as Steam-A-Seam or Wonder-Under.

Bo-Nash Bonding Powder

Sold as Bo-Nash Bonding Agent 007, this invisible fusible powder has many uses. It's perfect for adhering fabric to fabric, especially when working with delicate materials such as lace or tulle. Simply sprinkle the powder onto the receiving fabric, position your second fabric over it, then cover with a protective ironing sheet (we recommend the Bo-Nash Ironing & Craft Sheet) and fuse by pressing with a hot iron. Stitching or machine quilting can give added reinforcement.

The powder can also be used to hold bits and pieces—such as fabric snippets, paper scraps or even glitter—in place on a surface. Layer powder and material as needed to achieve the look you want. Or, sprinkle it on regular batting to make it fusible. Bo-Nash bonding powder can even come to the rescue for repairing fabrics. We have used it to apply a patch to a torn bed sheet, which has been laundered several times since and holds fast.

Spray Adhesives

Among other uses, spray adhesives are very helpful for holding quilt layers together in preparation for quilting. These sprays eventually dissipate or dissolve in the wash, so they do not form a permanent bond. You can reposition the fabric

This elephant mobile was made using Floriani's double-sided fusible Stitch N Shape. Visit www.loveinstitches.com for downloadable instructions to make this project.

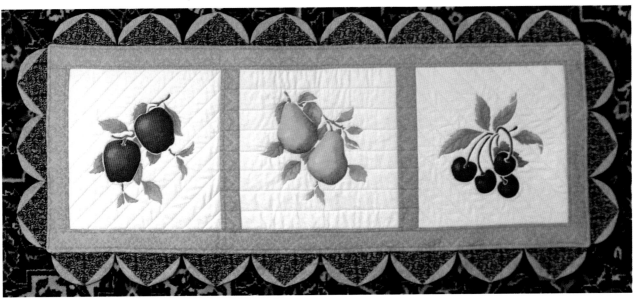

In the quilted creation "Delectable Fruit," the fruits were painted using freezer paper stencils.

by simply pulling it away from the batting and smoothing it down again. Steaming the "quilt sandwich" lightly with an iron will secure and smooth the layers.

There are many brands available, such as Generations™ Quilt Basting Spray (by Sullivans USA), Sulky® KK 2000, 3M™ Basting Spray and J.T. Trading's 505® Spray and Fix. J.T. Trading also makes 606® Spray and Fix, which makes any fabric, batting, paper or stabilizer into a fusible product. Simply spray it on the back of the appliqué pieces, let it dry and then heat-set the pieces in place with an iron when ready. It works for applying fabric to fabric as well as paper to fabric, and the bond created is permanent.

Fusible Grid

We know of two fusible grid brands: June Tailor's Quilt Top Express™, available in packages, and Pellon's Tru-Grid™, sold in packages or by the yard. A grid is especially handy when you need to duplicate, alter or scale up a pattern, or you can use one to help you place items uniformly. Quilters have been known to use grids for creating watercolor backgrounds, quilted photography and postage-stamp quilts.

Fusible Tape

Fusible tape is useful for holding hems, binding, ribbons and trims in place while sewing. It's available in many brands, such as Steam-A-Seam and HeatnBond, and most come in both ¼" and ½" versions. A mini-iron is the tool of choice in working with these narrow fusible tapes.

Fusible Thread

Superior Threads makes Charlotte's Fusible Web™, a thread designed by Charlotte Warr Andersen, that can be used in various ways. Charlotte has advocated its use for preparing appliqué pieces and for applying binding to quilts, because it provides a light bond with great adhesion.

Freezer Paper

Freezer paper has become a staple in many quilters' and crafters' tool boxes. Its uses are varied, and it is inexpensive and easy to use. We have used it for making stencils to paint on fabric and to stabilize appliqué pieces for machine or hand appliqué.

Affixed to the inside edge using a mini-iron, this ¼" fusible tape will help hold the binding in place as it is being sewn.

9

Fusible Embellishments

Fusible Bias Tape

Pre-made Quick Bias fusible tape made by Clover irons on and comes in ¼" and ⅛" widths and a variety of solid and marble colors, including metallic gold and silver, as well as four variegated colors. Because this tape is produced from bias fabric and already has the fusible on the back, it is easily ironed onto straight or curved designs. It eliminates time spent making custom bias tape and pinning it in place. It is easy to maneuver, using a mini-iron, and is repositionable when re-heated.

Most quilters are familiar with the Celtic and stained glass designs that can be done with this handy embellishment. Try weaving it as a back-ground fabric, fusing that to a base and creating purses or embellished wearables. Use it to frame quilt squares or borders for an added touch of color. Scrapbookers can use the tape to make frames in a snap.

Fusible Ribbon and Decorative Thread

Hot Ribbon Art©, available in many colors, is ideal for crafts, quilting, appliqué, clothing, scrap-booking and doll-making. Only ⅛" wide, it can be fused to give delicate enhancement to designs on fabric or paper. Experiment with this versatile trim on all types of fabrics, paper, wood, card-board, cork and papier-mâché. The manufacturer, Imagination International, Inc., provides excellent guidelines for the use of this product.

Kreinik iron-on threads, including Finishing Touches carded thread sets, come in many colors and thicknesses. When applying this embellish-ment to any project, using a mini-iron affords you better control when placing and fusing the thread.

Fusible Crystals, Nailheads and Other Adornments

Kandi Corp. makes crystals (including Swarovski®), rhinestones, pearls and metal nail-heads and studs (including the Brass It Up™ line) for the crafter to embellish and add sparkle to

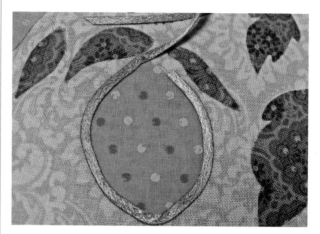

Fusible ribbon can be used to create elements or enhance existing ones.

their creations. These fusible products are also used in quilting with great success. These embel-lishments can be affixed to a variety of surfaces using an iron or a hot-fix applicator wand. When heat is applied to the embellishment, the glue on the back of it melts, adhering it to the surface.

Fusible Synthetic Suede

Kandi Corp. makes Zwade™, an imitation suede product with fusible on the back. Available in eighteen colors, it can be cut or punched to shape and quickly fused to many surfaces.

Angelina® Fibers

These very fine fibers differ from other metal-lic threads in that they maintain a soft hand, even when fused. They come in many colors and different textures and can be found in iri-descent, holographic, metallized and electric shades. The product is also environmentally friendly. Approximately twenty colors offered are fusible (fiber to fiber) to create unique Angelina fabric. Other threads, ribbons and scraps can be trapped between the layers of Angelina, and then the entire new fabric can be stitched or fused to a background fabric (or paper) using Bo-Nash bonding powder or another fusible product.

Other Fusibles

Printable Fabric Sheets

Printable fabric sheets are readily available in craft, hobby and quilting stores. We like June Tailor Quick Fuse™ inkjet fabric sheets, which provide wonderful, good-quality printed images. In addition, it has the advantage of having the fusible already on the backside, creating endless possibilities for fusing to other fabrics, paper or wood items.

No-Sew Shade Kit

June Tailor has been producing this kit for many years, allowing the home user to choose fabric to create custom window shades, minus the sewing. The kit includes everything you need (except your chosen fabric) to be successful, even some templates for creating decorative bottom edges for the shades. Detailed instructions and accessories to create one shade are included in each kit.

Fusible Velcro

This addition to the Velcro® line of products allows non-sewers to fuse closures to paper/fabric combination projects, such as the paper dolls we have designed for this book. Fusing the Velcro to paper-backed clothes that attach to the fusible fleece on the front of the dolls made for quick and easy clothing outfit changes. Use it on other items that are not easy to sew regular Velcro onto.

Iron-On Vinyl

Manufactured by Therm O Web, this product comes in two finishes: Lustre (gloss) for a shiny, brilliant look and Matte for a non-glossy, satin look. This fusible vinyl provides a durable, scuff-resistant and water-resistant finish. Among its many uses, this product can be used to protect memorabilia, mount dried flowers, protect place mats or coasters, make bibs and cover books.

Barbara redid her kitchen windows by creating new shades and matching valances with the June Tailor No-Sew Shade Kit. Pictured are Gary and Pamela, the authors' support team.

Patterns printed on Quick Fuse fabric sheets are affixed to a wooden box for the project on page 60.

FOR MORE INFO

See "Resources" on page 126 for additional information on the manufacturers of the fusibles used in this book, plus where to find some of the non-fusible products that are specific to certain projects.

Essential Tools for Fusing

Before fusing, you will need to gather the appropriate tools for the job.

Small Travel Iron

On many of the book's projects, a small iron is preferable to fuse in tight places. They are more maneuverable than a full-size iron, and easy to handle and store. Two we recommend are Rowenta's DA35 Compact Iron and Clover's Compact Craft Iron. Both fold flat and come with travel cases.

Mini-Iron

A mini-iron is useful for fusing small items, such as bias tapes and decorative threads, and for fusing in hard-to-reach areas. Several are sold with interchangeable tips, increasing their versatility. Two brands we recommend that make excellent starter kits are Clover's Mini Iron II™ The Adapter Set and the Creative Textile Tool™ by Walnut Hollow®. In addition to the standard large and small triangular tips, these kits come with a variety of tips for such tasks as sealing inner edges and shaping three-dimensional objects. Check the manufacturers' websites for more details on the tips included.

A mini-iron is a must for small jobs, including tight areas and precision work.

Hot-Fix Applicator Wand

We tested two brands that we can recommend for fusing crystals, metal studs or other small iron-on embellishments onto a project. The Kandi Kane™, a mid-range applicator made by Kandi Corp., is easily found in most hobby or craft stores. It comes with eight tips: six concave ones to fit specific crystal sizes, plus two flat-tip sizes. Some people prefer the added control of the concave tips for placing the crystals. Walnut Hollow's Designed for Her™ Creative Jewel Tool™ comes with three flat tips and tweezers for placing the crystals.

Pressing Sheets

Pressing sheets protect your iron from picking up residue as a result of fusing. They are also useful for fusible appliqué in particular, as you can create your fused piece directly on the sheet, then peel it off and apply it to the receiving surface.

Pressing sheets come in many brands and sizes, in several different finishes. The Bo-Nash Giant Non-Stick Ironing & Craft Sheet, a 12" × 18" fiberglass sheet coated with Teflon®, was one of the best we tried for protecting irons and ironing surfaces. Clean the sheet with a nylon kitchen scrubber after each use to keep any stray glue from adhering to the surface of your next project. If you do get sticky residue on your iron, a Bo-Nash Ironslide Iron Clean Sheet is helpful for restoring its surface.

Kreinik makes Adhesive Teflon Press Cloth that sticks directly to your mini-iron to protect it. You might prefer this when you'd rather not have to deal with using or trimming down a large pressing sheet.

Spray Booth

When working with spray adhesives (or spray paint), it is helpful to set up a spray booth with a raised grid inside to keep the appliqué pieces from flipping over while applying adhesive. It also works to keep overspray (both adhesive and paint) contained. You can make one by placing a screen, netting or rack in a cardboard box.

Fusing Hints

Here are some important things to keep in mind for successful (and safe) fusing.

Before Fusing

- Set up your workspace so that all the tools and materials you need are at your fingertips.
- Follow the recommended warm-up times for your fusing tools. Preheating your iron properly will help ensure that materials hold once fused.
- Read the manufacturer's instructions for each fusible product you use, including the recommended time and temperature for fusing. Don't assume that all similar products work in the exact same way!
- Prep your materials properly for fusing: clean receiving surfaces, and wash fabrics beforehand as directed. The fusible product instructions will tell you how to get the best results.
- Fuse on scrap fabric before starting any final piece, to test compatibility between the fusible and the type of fabric or paper you are using.
- When selecting the right fusible batting, web, interfacing or stabilizer for a fabric project, consider (1) its thickness, for achieving the feel or drape you want; (2) how easy the material is to sew through; (3) its color and whether it will be visible from the other side once attached.
- When using fusible web, which is applied to the back of your fabric rather than the front, you must reverse asymmetrical designs so they will look as intended on the finished piece.

During and After Fusing

- DO NOT touch any metal portion of an iron or applicator tool while in use. They can get very hot and cause severe burns.
- Always be aware of the position of your heated applicator tools and irons. It is easy to be careless and reach across a hot iron.
- When using double-stick adhesive such as Steam-A-Seam 2, always trace on the side where the paper does NOT come off as readily.
- Never iron on the glue side of any applicable fusible product, only the paper side.

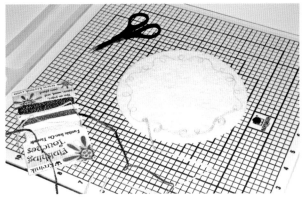

A tempered glass mat (like this one made by Walnut Hollow) provides a safe, flat workspace for cutting and working with hot fusing tools.

Juliet Campbell, age 7, prepares to fuse a ballerina (from StenSource®) onto fabric, with mom Diane's help. Kids can fuse, too, but should only do so with close adult supervision.

- Don't glide the iron, but rather press it down on your material when fusing.
- Protect your irons and your fused creations by using Teflon pressing sheets and/or adhesive Teflon. Clean pressing sheets routinely with a nylon kitchen scrubber.
- Always work in a well-ventilated area when using spray adhesives (and spray paints, too) and wear a painter's breathing mask. This is very important in avoiding damage to your respiratory system.
- When deciding if a fused piece such as a quilt needs supplemental stitching, consider whether it will be washed or handled much, and could use the added reinforcement. You might also want to stitch for a more finished look.

Fusing Technique Projects

In this section are simple, fun step-by-step projects to teach basic use of the most common fusible products. Since one of us is a quilter and the other an artist and crafter, we were able to explore paper, wood, metal and fabric in many different types of applications. Quilting and sewing projects appear first, followed by those that cross over between sewing and crafting and any we deem more suitable for crafters. Fabric is used in all.

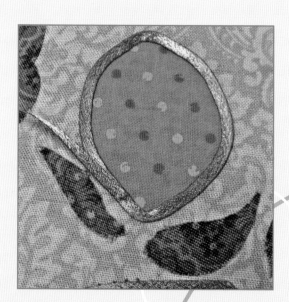

Spinning Rainbow Quilt

Finished size: 18" diameter

For those quilters who may be challenged when it comes to paper-piecing, try backing the pattern pieces with fusible web before arranging them on a base fabric, and then fuse the pieces in place. Because we are tracing the exact shapes and fusing them into their final position, there is no seam allowance, so the edges of all the fused pieces will be "raw." You can stitch them down with a decorative stitch for a more finished look. All pieces will lay flat in the center, important if you intend to use this quilt as a table mat.

Materials

▶ Fusing Supplies:

2 yd. paper-backed fusible web

¼" Steam-A-Seam 2 fusible tape

Temporary basting spray or
  Bo-Nash bonding powder

▶ Other Materials:

Fat eighth (9" × 22") light gray
(for background fabric)

(1) 8" square each of 9 rainbow colors
(for pinwheel)

(3) 9" square each of 3 gray/black prints
(for border)

(2) 2" × 40" strips striped fabric (for binding)

22" square base fabric (muslin or batiste)

22" square backing fabric

22" square Warm & Natural® batting

Coordinating threads (for decorative stitching)

▶ Tools and Templates:

Inkjet printer

Permanent marker

Rotary cutter and mat

Ruler

Iron and mini-iron

Teflon pressing sheet

Basic sewing supplies

Templates from the CD: SpinRainbow

Make Final Cuts Easy and Exact

A rotary cutter and ruler make it easy to get straight lines when making the final cuts of these geometric shapes. Scissors can be used, but be careful to cut all lines straight and exactly on the drawn line.

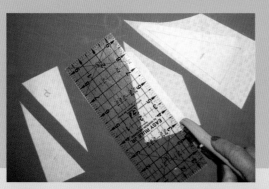

Prepare the Quilt Pieces

1 Print the templates.

2 Trace nine of each shape (large triangle, small triangle, trapezoid) on the paper side of the fusible web.

3 Loosely cut the individual shapes apart, leaving at least ¼" around the outside edges of all shapes.

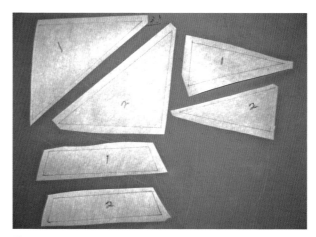

Template shapes traced onto fusible web and loosely cut.

4 With your iron, fuse all the small triangles to the wrong side of the light gray background fabric. Cut out the shapes along the traced lines.

5 Fuse three trapezoids each to the wrong sides of the three gray/black prints. Cut out the shapes. You could use just one fabric for the border, but varying shades add interest.

6 Fuse a large triangle to the wrong side of each rainbow-color print, for a total of nine. Cut out the shapes.

Position the Pieces and Fuse in Place

1 Peel off the paper from the fused fabric shapes. Arrange the large triangles in a pinwheel formation on the base fabric. We used white batiste as our base, as it is lightweight and didn't add extra bulk to the finished quilt.

2 Position the small light gray background triangles, then the gray/black border pieces.

3 Once you are happy with your layout, fuse the pieces in place, following the manufacturer's instructions for time and temperature, and using the Teflon pressing sheet to protect the iron.

The quilt seams stitched.

Trim the Edges and Bind

1 Once the quilting is complete, use a rotary cutter and ruler to trim all the edges of the quilt even with the gray/black border. Bind the quilt as desired. We cut two 2" × 40" binding strips and attached the binding to the front with a ¼" seam, mitering the corners.

The quilt pieces fused in place.

Add Batting, Backing and Stitching

1 Layer the fused piece with batting and backing, and baste to secure the layers for quilting. We used a temporary basting spray, but you could also use Bo-Nash bonding powder or specially purchased fusible batting.

2 Decide on either a zigzag or decorative stitch and begin to stitch the "seams" of the fused piece to permanently secure them to the quilt. At this time you will also be creating the quilted texture of the piece.

Quilt edges trimmed and binding attached.

For Quilting Basics

If you're uncertain about any of the quilting techniques used in some of the projects—or if you need some basic quilting lessons—come to www.loveinstitches.com and click on Barbara's Quilting Basics.

2 After pressing the binding flat, turn the quilt over and fuse ¼" SAS2 tape to the back edges with a mini-iron.

3 Fold down the taped edges and press in place, just covering the original stitching line. This helps to hold the binding in place as you stitch in the ditch from the front, catching the edge of the binding in the back. This technique creates a nice machine-stitched binding on both sides in no time at all.

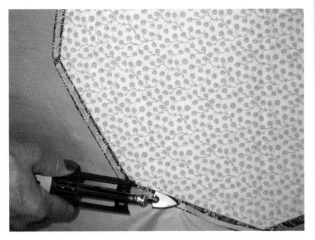

Fusing iron-on adhesive tape to the back edges.

The finished back.

GALLERY

Even complicated designs like this one, made by Barbara, can be simplified with fusing.

Finished size: 19" diameter

Margo Rose, quilt pattern designer and owner of Future Heirlooms, fused this pattern, "Ambrosius," avoiding some tedious and intricate piecing. (www.future-heirlooms.com)

Finished size: 24" square

Fusing made this creation, "Spinning Pinwheels," easier for quilt artist Sara Moe to complete. Sara is well-known for her unique curved quilt block designs and curved piecing techniques. (www.sewinspired.com)

Finished size: 33" square

Four-Way Heart Appliqué Quilt

Finished size: 33" × 12"

> *Stitching this sampler will give you a feel for basic fusing techniques. One heart pattern is fused four different ways to machine appliqué it to a background fabric. When you add sashing and binding, you have a charming piece for baby's wall or for decorating on Valentine's Day.*

Materials

Fusing Supplies:

Paper-backed fusible web (non-woven)

Temporary adhesive spray

Floriani's No Show Nylon Mesh Fusible, or any woven fusible interfacing with glue on one side

Charlotte's Fusible Web thread

14" × 36" piece June Tailor Quilter's Fusible Batting

Fusible fleece (optional)

Other Materials:

(4) 4" squares red fabric

(4) 7" squares background fabric

Tear-away or wash-away stabilizer

⅜ yd. pebble fabric (for inner borders, sashing and binding)

1 yd. red fabric (for outer borders and backing)

MonoPoly™ (monofilament polyester) invisible thread (Note: Do NOT use a nylon invisible thread; it will melt on your iron.)

Coordinating threads (for sewing and quilting)

Tools and Templates:

Inkjet printer

Tracing paper

Extra-fine permanent marker

Iron

Miracle Chalk Chubby Crayon or other chalk marker

Basic sewing supplies

Templates from the CD: Cards (heart shape only)

Basic Instructions for All Four Appliqué Methods

1 Read all instructions before beginning this project.

2 Print out the heart template from the CD and prepare each heart appliqué using one of the four methods.

3 Find the center of the 7" background square by folding it in half vertically and horizontally, then pressing.

4 Center the heart on the background square and fuse in place.

5 Put a tear-away or wash-away stabilizer on the back side of the square and use a satin, blanket, decorative or zigzag stitch around all the outside edges to secure the appliqué.

6 Remove the stabilizer.

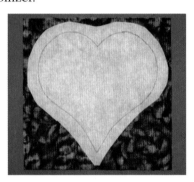

Fusible-web heart fused to the red square.

Basic Fusible-Web Appliqué

1 Trace the printed heart on the paper side of the fusible web, using the permanent marker.

2 Loosely cut out the heart, leaving at least ¼" around the outside edge.

3 Fuse this shape to the wrong side of one 4" red square.

4 Cut out the shape along the traced line.

5 Follow steps 3 and 4 of the Basic Instructions to fuse the heart to the background square.

6 Follow steps 5 and 6 of the Basic Instructions to secure the fused appliqué.

The cut-out heart.

Donut-Style Fusible-Web Appliqué

1 Trace the heart on the paper side of the fusible web, using the permanent marker.

2 Loosely cut out the heart, leaving at least ¼" around the outside edge.

3 Cut out the inside of the heart shape, ¼" from the drawn line.

Donut-style, fusible-web heart fused to the red square.

4 Fuse this "donut" heart shape to the wrong side of one 4" red square.

5 Cut carefully along the traced line and follow steps 3 and 4 of the Basic Instructions on page 22 to fuse the heart to the background. If a trapunto (or raised) effect is desired, trace the heart onto a piece of fusible fleece. Cut ⅜" inside the line and fuse the fleece to the back of the heart before fusing the heart to the backing fabric.

6 Follow steps 5 and 6 of the Basic Instructions to secure the fused appliqué.

The heart cut out along the traced line.

Woven Fusible Interfacing Appliqué

1 Trace the heart onto a piece of tracing paper, using the permanent marker.

2 Trim off the excess tracing paper, leaving a border of at least 1" around the outside edge.

3 Lightly spray the back side of the tracing with temporary adhesive spray before laying it on the No Show Nylon Mesh (or other woven fusible interfacing), to keep the paper from shifting.

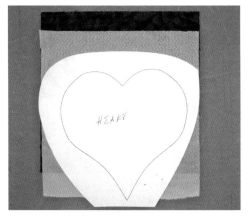

The red square, interfacing and tracing paper layered.

4 Layer the 4" red square (right side up), the fusible interfacing (fusible side down), and top with the sprayed tracing-paper pattern (glue side down). Pin to keep all the layers together.

5 Sew on the drawn line, using a short stitch length. Remove the tracing paper by carefully pulling it away. The small stitch length should make this task easy.

The heart stitched and the tracing paper removed.

6　Trim ⅛" from the stitched line, along all curves and into the point of the heart.

7　Snip a small slit in the interfacing, and turn the heart right side out. This will put the glue side of the interfacing on the outside now.

8　Use a stylus or another pointed tool to push out all the edges. Finger press to smooth the shape.

9　Follow steps 3 and 4 of the Basic Instructions on page 22 to fuse the heart to the background. If desired, stuff a little fiberfill or a small piece of batting into the opening before fusing in place to create a puffy heart.

10　Follow steps 5 and 6 of the Basic Instructions to secure the fused appliqué.

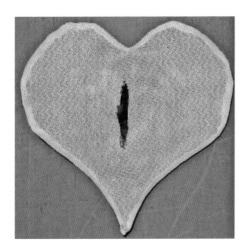

A slit cut in the interfacing allows the heart to be turned right side out.

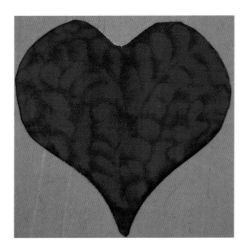

Fusible Thread Appliqué

1　Trace the heart on the right side of the 4" red square, using a chalk marker (we used Miracle Chalk Chubby Crayon, which disappears once heat is applied). Note: Do not use a water-soluble marker, as heat may set this in the fabric permanently.

2　Wind the bobbin on your sewing machine with Charlotte's Fusible Web, and thread the machine with MonoPoly invisible thread.

3　Stitch around the traced pattern line. You may have to adjust the tension on the sewing machine to get a stitching line that lays flat, with no puckering.

4　Trim close to stitching line and follow steps 3 and 4 of the Basic Instructions on page 22 to fuse the heart to the background. Use a dry iron and be quick and firm (10 seconds or less), as steam may cause the work to shrivel and too much heat can cause the thread to shrink. Note: This is only a temporary bond that will hold the appliqué in place until the final stitching is done. You can remove the invisible thread while the piece is still warm, if you wish.

5　Follow steps 5 and 6 of the Basic Instructions to secure the fused appliqué.

The heart is fused only along its edges in this technique.

Quilt Finishing Instructions

1 Trim all blocks to 6½".

2 From the pebble fabric, cut two 1¾" × 30½" pieces and five 1¾" × 6½" pieces for the inner borders and sashing. Cut three 2" × 40" pieces for the binding.

3 From the red fabric, cut two 2" × 30½" pieces for the side outer borders and two 2" × 12½" pieces for the top and bottom borders.

4 Sew the blocks, sashing and borders as shown in the photo on page 21 to assemble the quilt top.

5 Cut a piece of backing from the red fabric to measure 14" × 36".

6 Layer the backing, fusible batting and the quilt top and fuse the layers together to baste.

7 Quilt as desired. The quilt pictured was echo-quilted around all the hearts and stitched in the ditch around all borders and blocks.

8 Bind using Charlotte's Fusible Web in the bobbin. Sew the binding onto the back of the quilt.

9 Turn the quilt over and press the binding in position, just covering the fusible thread. The fusible thread will hold the binding in place temporarily.

10 Stitch the binding down from the front of the quilt using MonoPoly invisible thread and a zigzag stitch, if you prefer an invisible look. To add another decorative element to the quilt, you can use a coordinating thread and a decorative machine stitch. This stitching will capture all the binding and quilt layers securely.

11 Add a hanging sleeve, if desired.

Detail of the finished quilt.

Choose the Fusing Method That Fits

Try the woven fusible interfacing technique if you prefer to hand-appliqué your blocks, as the material retains a very soft hand. By stitching the pieces right-sides together and then turning the appliqué right side out, the edges are all turned under and fused in place for the hand-stitching process.

For wearables and bed quilts, use the woven fusible interfacing technique, or try the fusible thread technique. Since the appliqué is only fused around the outside edges, you can cut away the background fabric from behind it, if desired, to reduce bulk.

Fusible web tends to make the finished project a little stiffer, which may be beneficial for a wall hanging to give it additional support.

One-Heart Gridded Quilt

Finished size: 24" square

We had fun choosing fabrics from all of Yolanda's fabric designs for this pattern. Search your stash to find coordinating prints in any color that will complement your individual style. This design can be contemporary, traditional or primitive, for baby, teenager, mom or grandma depending on your color and fabric choices. A fusible grid will help you keep the many squares of the background in line as you work.

Materials

▶ ## Fusing Supplies:

27" square fusible, non-woven 1" grid (June Tailor or Pellon)

11" × 16" piece paper-backed fusible web (non-woven)

27" square fusible batting

▶ ## Other Materials:

(8 or 9) 2" × 40" strips assorted green prints (for background)

Fat quarter bright red print (for heart)

¼ yd. red print (for borders)

¼ yd. red print (for binding)

¾ yd. backing fabric

Coordinating threads (for piecing and quilting)

▶ ## Tools and Templates:

Inkjet printer

Permanent marker

Rotary cutter and mat

Iron

Teflon pressing sheet

Large pressing surface

Basic sewing supplies

Thick bath towels (optional)

Templates from the CD: OneHeart

Cut Your Fabric

1 Cut two 3½" × 18½" strips and two 3½" × 24½" strips of red border print.

2 Cut three 2" × 40" strips of the red binding print.

3 Cut one hundred and forty-four 2" squares from the assorted green prints. Note: We used a fat quarter and cut the binding on the bias to feature the striped print on the diagonal.

Arrange and Fuse the Squares

1 Randomly arrange the 2" green squares onto a 24" section of the grid, making sure to put them on the side with the glue.

2 When happy with your arrangement, use an iron and a Teflon pressing sheet to fuse in place, following the manufacturer's instructions for time and temperature. If you don't have an ironing surface that is large enough to place your 24" grid design, you can improvise with a few thick bath towels on any flat surface.

Arranging the squares on the fusible grid.

Yolanda fusing with an iron and a Teflon pressing sheet.

Sew the Seams and Seam Allowances

1 Fold the right sides together along the first vertical line between the squares and sew a scant ¼" seam allowance. Continue sewing all vertical seams along the grid lines between the squares.

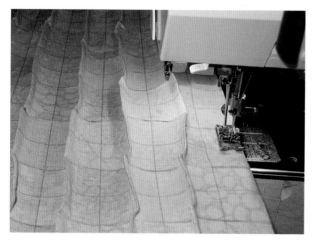

Sewing the vertical seams.

2 When all the seams are sewn, clip ¼" in the seam allowances where the squares intersect.

3 Press the seam allowances in alternating directions.

4 Fold and sew the horizontal seam allowances, making sure to nestle the opposing seam allowances to avoid bulk.

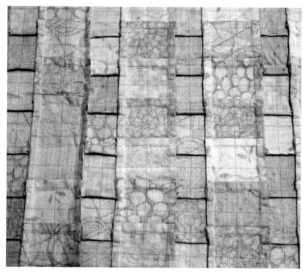

The back view of all seams and seam allowances sewn.

5 When all seams are sewn, press the quilt top from the front.

The pressed quilt squares.

Add the Heart

1 Print the heart halves on two sheets of paper and tape them together, lining up the dotted lines.

2 Trace one half of the heart onto the paper side of the fusible web. Flip it over on the "fold" line and trace the other side. Fuse this web to the wrong side of the red heart fabric. Cut carefully along the traced line.

3 Remove the paper backing, center on the quilt top and fuse in place.

The heart appliqué fused onto the quilt.

Clean Your Pressing Sheet

When repositioning the Teflon pressing sheet, first clean off any fusible debris from the sheet with a nylon kitchen scrubber to avoid getting any fusible web on the front of your quilt.

Finish the Quilt

1 Trim the quilt top to measure 18½" square.

2 Sew two 18½" borders to the sides of the quilt. Press and trim off any excess to square up the sides. Sew the remaining two borders to the top and bottom.

3 Layer the backing, fusible batting and quilt top, and fuse in place.

4 Quilt as desired. Ours was quilted across the diagonal lines of the squares and into the borders. The heart was sewn with a buttonhole stitch during the quilting process to secure it and quilt it in the same step. Additional lines of echo quilting were done on the inside of the heart.

5 Trim to square up your top and bind with the 2" strips of red print, using your favorite binding method.

The borders and binding added.

GALLERY

Another method for creating a pieced background using fusibles was performed by art quilter and horticulturist Sue Andrus. For her "Antique Irises and Tulips," she pieced the background by fusing many different ivory fabrics to small-to-medium batting pieces, and satin-stitched the pieces together. She then arranged the flower appliqués in various ways over the background before deciding on the final arrangement. (www.andrusgardensquilts.com)

Finished size: 26" × 24"

A Different Spin Wall Hanging

Finished size: 24" square

Use two different color strips to showcase the woven fabric. This is a great way to create texture and excitement when you need a background for any appliqué motif. With this wall hanging, we created the "weave" with cotton fabrics, than appliquéd with wool.

Materials

▶ **Fusing Supplies:**

24" square fusible batting

606 Spray and Fix

Freezer paper

▶ **Other Materials:**

⅝ yd. medium green tonal fabric
(for woven strips and binding)

½ yd. green lace print (for border)

⅜ yd. ivory brocade
(for woven strips and binding)

¾ yd. backing fabric

Wool scraps for appliqué in colors of choice

Coordinating threads
(for piecing and stitching appliqué)

▶ **Tools and Templates:**

Iron

Teflon pressing sheet

Spray booth

Tracing paper

Basic sewing supplies

Templates from the CD: WoolApplique1,
WoolApplique2

A pinking-edge blade puts a decorative edge on the strips to be woven.

Cut the Appliqué Pieces

1 Print the templates directly onto sheets of freezer paper, or print on regular paper and then trace onto the freezer paper.

2 Iron the freezer-paper patterns to the wool to cut the appliqué pieces. Remember to iron with "shiny" side of freezer paper to the fabric. Since the two sides of this design mirror each other, you can use one freezer-paper pattern for each side by simply pressing it to the front of the wool for one side and the back of the wool for the other.

Cut Your Fabric

1 From the medium green tonal print and ivory brocade, cut seven 1½" × 40" strips each. Use a pinking-edge blade on your rotary cutter if desired.

2 From the medium green tonal print, cut three 2" × 40" strips for binding

3 From the green lace print, cut two 3½" × 18½" strips and two 3½" × 24" strips for the binding.

4 From the dark green brocade, cut two 3½" × 18½" strips and two 3½" × 24" strips for the border.

5 From the backing fabric, cut one 24" square.

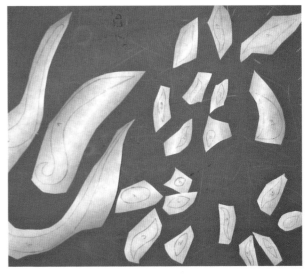

Appliqué patterns printed or traced onto freezer paper.

Weave (Assemble) the Background

1 Mark the fusible batting 3" from all outside edges to create an inner square of 18".

2 Line up the green strips on the diagonal, cutting them as needed to cover an area just larger than the drawn square.

Green strips lined up diagonally on the fusible batting.

3 Begin weaving in the ivory strips by lifting back every other green strip and laying an ivory one across. Return the lifted green strips to their original placement, then lift the alternate green strips. Repeat this process until all ivory strips are "woven" with the green strips, cutting the strips as needed.

Weaving in the ivory strips.

Fused background, with two of the four borders attached.

Fuse the Background

1 Once all the strips are in place, fuse the entire woven piece with an iron up to the edge of the drawn line.

2 Turn the piece batting-side up and fold back one side to the drawn line. Trim the excess fabric strips to the line. Repeat for the other three sides.

3 Turn the piece fabric-side up and carefully pin and sew the two 18½" border strips to opposite sides (right sides together). Trim, if needed, and attach the last two borders. Press back and fuse in place on the batting.

Add Backing and Stitching

1 Fuse the backing onto the quilt and trim the piece to square it up.

2 Stitch in the ditch between the quilt top and the border, and then ⅛" in from the outside edge to secure the quilt and bind it, using the three 2" ivory brocade strips.

3 Quilt across the diagonal rows of the woven strips, if desired. This step may not be necessary if using as a wall hanging (see sidebar on page 33).

Stitching on the background.

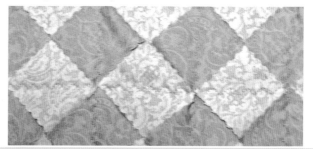

Attach the Appliqué

1 Set up a spray booth (see page 12) and spray the back side of all the pieces with the 606 Spray and Fix, following the manufacturer's instructions.

2 Make a tracing of the finished design to help you place the pieces. You only have to trace one side and the center motifs. Mark the center horizontal and vertical lines of your quilt top and fold the tracing in half both horizontally and vertically to find the center of the layout. Pin the tracing so that the placement of the right side is showing, then position the pieces. Remove the tracing paper and fuse using a pressing sheet.

3 Flip over the tracing and pin it so that the placement is showing for the left side, and finish the design.

4 Use a buttonhole or zigzag stitch to sew around all raw edges, if desired (see sidebar). This will quilt the piece as it secures the appliqué. You may want to do some additional quilting in the background and borders and some satin or zigzag stitching to create the stems.

After the appliqué pieces are placed on one half, flip over the traced pattern to guide placement on other half.

No-Sew Appliqué

If this piece will be used as a wall hanging and you don't think it will be washed or handled much, you don't have to stitch down the fused wool pieces. The only sewing in the entire project, then, would involve attaching the borders and stitching on the binding.

Diamond-and-Lace Christmas Quilt

Block size: 17" × 10"
Finished size: 20" × 34"

> *Yolanda brought back some wonderful handmade lace from a trip to Belgium. Bonding powder provided the perfect medium for attaching the lace to this simple yet charming quilt.*

Materials

▶ **Fusing Supplies:**

Bo-Nash bonding powder

22" × 36" piece fusible batting

▶ **Other Materials:**

2 different fat quarters red fabric

2 different fat quarters green fabric

1 yd. coordinating fabric
(for backing and binding)

3 lace or other appliqué motifs
(approximately 9" × 6")

Coordinating threads

Monofilament invisible thread (optional)

▶ **Tools:**

Iron

Teflon pressing sheet

Water-filled spray bottle

Freezer paper

Ruler

Rotary cutter and mat

Basic sewing supplies

Cut Your Fabric

1 From the coordinating fabric, cut one 22" × 36" piece for the backing, and three 2" strips for the binding.

2 From each of the red fabrics, cut four 9⅝" × 5⅝" rectangles. Recut two of each color square on the diagonal from bottom left to upper right, and two from bottom right to upper left (see photo).

3 From each of the green fabrics, cut two 9⅝" × 5⅝" rectangles. Recut one of each square on the opposite diagonals, the same as the red rectangles.

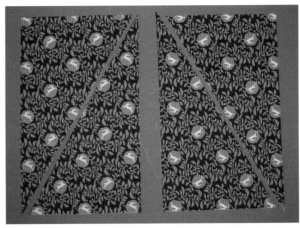

A set of red triangles that will form one of the diamonds.

Sew Together the Triangles

1 Referring to the photo, sew together two different green triangles. Press open and trim the points. Repeat to make a total of four units.

2 Repeat with the red triangles for a total of eight units.

Sewing together different patterns in the same color, forming one of the four sections that make up each quilt block.

3 Lay out the pieced units as shown in the photo and assemble the blocks.

4 Join the blocks together to complete the quilt top.

Finish the Quilt

1 Layer the backing, batting and top, and baste by fusing together.

2 Quilt as desired. The quilt shown was stitched in the ditch around the diamonds and between the blocks, then echo-quilted around the diamonds.

3 Use the 2" strips to bind the finished quilt as desired.

Fuse the Lace Motifs

1 Sprinkle the Bo-Nash bonding powder generously on a piece of freezer paper.

2 Spray the wrong side of each lace appliqué lightly with water, and place the wet side down onto the powder.

3 Lift, shake off the excess powder, and place each appliqué on the quilt top.

4 Using the pressing sheet to protect your iron, press until a good fuse is achieved, on high heat.

5 If desired, use a monofilament invisible thread to sew around the main body of each appliqué to secure them. We've found that the bonding powder used alone provides a really good fuse for lace, so we didn't feel the need to stitch it down. We did stitch around the outside edges of the lace to provide additional quilting to the diamond centers.

The assembled background, before finishing.

36

Philosophical Chicken Tea Cozy

Finished size: 10" × 14"

Much fusing experimentation was taking place in Yolanda's studio when her friend, Marta McDowell, came to visit. A crafter herself, Marta caught the fusing "bug" and went home with all sorts of fusibles to try. A couple weeks later, she showed up with a double-sided piece showing a chicken on one side and a fried egg on the other. It was a new spin on the age-old question of which came first. In her joy at being able to appliqué layered wool pieces effortlessly, Marta had forgotten to address the problem of having both sides available to be seen. We arrived at a perfect solution—a tea cozy, complete with fusible fleece.

Marta's original, about which we can actually say: This came first.

Materials

▶ Fusing Supplies:

1 yd. paper-backed fusible web

(2) 12" × 18" pieces fusible fleece

2 yd. ¼" Steam-A-Seam 2 fusible tape

▶ Other Materials:

4 different fat quarters red and black fabrics, recut into 12" × 18" pieces

Fat quarter red fabric, cut into 2¼" bias strips for binding and pieced to measure at least 60"

(2) 12" × 18" pieces Insul-Bright® (insulating material)

Scraps of red, black, yellow, taupe and white prints

▶ Tools and Templates:

Inkjet printer

Rotary cutter and mat

Iron and mini-iron

Permanent marker

Basic sewing supplies

Templates from the CD: Chickenparts, FriedEgg, TeaCozy

Cut the Chicken and Egg Pieces

1 Print out the templates. The patterns have already been reversed, so the chicken and egg will finish as shown. The cozy pattern is only half. Print two patterns and tape them together to form the whole pattern.

2 Trace the chicken and egg pattern pieces onto the paper side of the fusible web, grouping shapes together that will go on like fabrics.

3 Loosely cut apart the pieces, leaving at least ¼" around the edges.

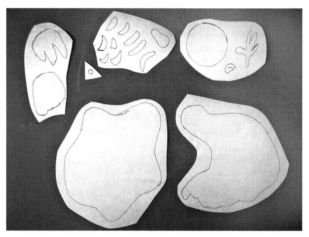

The chicken and egg pattern pieces, reversed as needed.

4 Remove the paper backing and place the fusible-web pattern pieces on the wrong side of the scrap fabrics, according to color. Fuse in place.

5 Cut out the fused pieces along the traced lines.

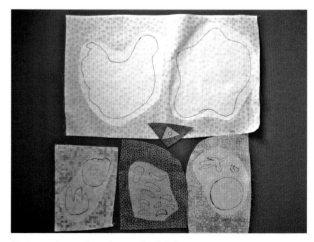

Pattern pieces fused onto the fabrics.

Prepare and Cut the Cozy

1 Layer one red 12" × 18" rectangle, right side up, on a piece of the Insul-Bright and quilt them using a crosshatch pattern.

2 Repeat for one 12" × 18" black rectangle and another piece of Insul-Bright.

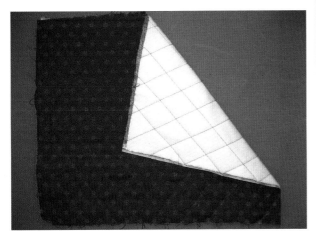

Red cozy fabric backed with Insul-Bright.

3 Fuse the other black 12" × 18" rectangle to a piece of fusible fleece, and repeat for the remaining red 12" × 18" rectangle and fusible fleece.

4 Trace around the tea cozy pattern with a permanent marker on each piece and cut out inside the line.

Pieced-together cozy template.

Fuse the Chicken and Egg Shapes onto the Cozy

1 Remove the paper backing from the egg and yolk. Center them on one of the red tea cozy shapes, and fuse in place.

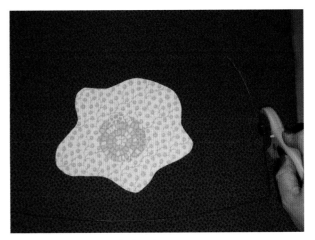

Cutting the cozy and placing the egg.

2 Repeat with one of the black tea cozy shapes and the chicken pattern pieces.

The chicken on the other side.

Finish the Cozy

1 Place the egg side of the tea cozy right side down. Layer the red quilted piece right side up, the black quilted piece right side down and the black chicken piece right side up.

The cozy's four layers.

2 Pin all the layers together carefully and sew through all thicknesses, using a ½" seam.

3 Prepare your bias binding strips and sew around the top of the assembled tea cozy, going from the bottom edge, around the top and back down to the bottom.

4 Press the binding back and, using a mini-iron, fuse the ¼" SAS2 tape on the inside edge of the binding. Remove the paper and fuse the binding to the inside, covering the stitching line. Stitch in the ditch from the right side, securing the binding.

5 Sew the bias binding to the bottom of the tea cozy, and follow the instructions above to finish sewing the binding to complete.

Fusing the tape on the binding's inside edge.

Folding and fusing the binding to cover the stitching line.

Crossover Projects

See page 116 to make a coordinating clock. The teapot design will work on the tea cozy as well.

Fusible fleece was used to create a trapunto effect for this set of wall hangings. Instructions and botanicals can be downloaded at www.loveinstitches.com.

Finished size (each panel): 7 " × 5½ "

Tabletop Holiday Tree

Finished size: 7½" × 6"

This petite charmer—which stands at just under eight inches, with the help of firm fusible stabilizer—can sit comfortably as an accent anywhere you would like a spot of cheer during the winter holidays. We even made it a tiny tree skirt. Reduced to half-size, they'd make really cute place cardholders for your holiday dinner table. The fabric used for this tree is by our friend, Sara Moe, who also fused on the decorative crystals.

Materials

▶ **Fusing Supplies:**

(2) 8" × 6¼" pieces Floriani Stitch N Shape double-sided fusible stabilizer

Fusible threads, ribbons and crystals (optional)

▶ **Other Materials:**

(2) 8" × 13" pieces coordinating fabric

Matching fabric or acrylic paint, for finishing edges (recommended)

▶ **Tools and Templates:**

Inkjet printer

Iron

Teflon pressing sheet

Heavy paper or cardstock, or template plastic

Fabric marker

Sharp-pointed, appliqué-style scissors

Templates from the CD: TabletopTree

Fuse the Fabric to the Stabilizer

1 Fold each of the two 8" × 13" pieces of fabrics in half lengthwise, wrong sides together, and iron flat.

2 Layer the fusible stabilizer inside one of the folded fabrics. Repeat with the other stabilizer and folded fabric.

The stabilizer layered inside the folded fabric.

3 Place each set of fabrics and stabilizers on an ironing surface. Cover with a pressing sheet and fuse down one side thoroughly, following the manufacturer's instructions. Turn it over and repeat for the other side. Check to make sure the fabric is fused securely to the stabilizer, pressing for additional time if needed.

Cut and Decorate the Interlocking Trees

1 Print the templates. We printed ours on heavier paper so they could be used repeatedly.

2 Cut out the templates and pin them in place on the fused fabric pieces to keep them from moving as you trace.

3 Trace the two different template shapes onto the fused fabric pieces and proceed to cut inside the traced lines. We prefer to make bold lines with a fabric marker so they can be seen easily, then take extra care while cutting so that the marker line gets cut away. You could also use a chalk pencil or water-soluble marker.

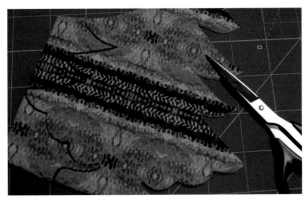

Cutting out one of the interlocking trees.

4 Once both halves of the tree are cut out, you may choose paint around the edges to hide the exposed white edge of the stabilizer. There are many ready-mix colors of acrylic or fabric paint available for you to choose from.

5 Slide together the interlocking pieces to make the tree stand up. If you want to decorate the tree further, apply fusible crystals, threads or ribbons. (See the projects on pages 52, 58, 60 and 64 for some application options.)

Pleated Broderie Perse Pillow

Finished size: 17" square

Broderie Perse hand appliqué, in which the chosen motif almost appears to be printed on the background fabric, was popular in the late 1800s. Today we can achieve the same effect with the convenience of fusing and machine stitching. Look for motifs that can be easily cut out. Different weights and textures of fabric add interest.

Materials

▶ **Fusing Supplies:**

Paper-backed fusible web, a piece large enough for the chosen motif

6" × 12" piece fusible woven interfacing

1½ yd. ¼" fusible bias tape

▶ **Other Materials:**

Floral motif of your choice (can be found in quilter's cottons or home decor fabrics)

12½" square base fabric

6" × 40" coordinating fabric (or same as base, for pleats)

⅓ yd. contrasting fabric (for corner triangles)

2" × 72" fabric strip (for piping)

2 yd. of ¼" cording

20" square backing fabric (for pillow back)

Monofilament invisible thread

16" pillow form

▶ **Tools:**

Iron

Teflon pressing sheet

Clotilde® Perfect Pleater™

Rotary cutter and mat

Ruler

Basic sewing supplies

Prepare the Pillow Front

1 Fuse the fusible web to the wrong side of the motif.

2 Carefully cut around the outside edges.

3 Remove the paper backing and fuse to the base fabric. We pieced four 6½" squares together to create our 12½" base.

4 Cut two 9½" squares of the contrasting fabric. Recut the squares diagonally for the four corner triangles.

Pillow front: the motif square with contrasting corners.

Create Pleated Pieces

1 Follow the pleater manufacturer's instructions for creating pleated fabric. Place the right side of the fabric down and use a thin tool to tuck the fabric down into the rows of the pleater.

2 Cut a piece of fusible woven interfacing the same size as the pleated fabric, and place the glue side down on the wrong side of the pleated fabric. Fuse in place, using a pressing sheet.

3 Turn over and carefully roll the pleater to remove the fabric.

Creating pleated fabric.

4 Trim one edge straight, and then cut pieces to your desired width. We cut four strips 1½" wide.

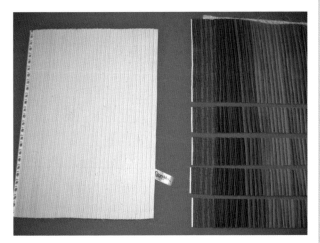

The pleater (left) and the trimmed, pleated fabric strips.

Piece Together the Pillow Front

1 Place one pleated strip along one side of the center square, right sides together. Place one corner triangle on top of this and pin all layers in place. Sew a ¼" seam.

2 Press the triangle and pleats to the outside, and repeat these steps for the other side.

3 Add the final two triangles and pleated strips to the remaining sides and press.

The pillow face after adding the pleats.

Finish the Pillow

1 Cut four 12" pieces of fusible bias tape. Fuse them to the outside edge of the pleated fabric and stitch to secure with a twin needle.

2 Stitch the motif with invisible thread, using a straight stitch around all the edges in a free-motion method.

3 Stitch down the bias tape on the pleated edge, using a twin needle.

4 Create the piping with cording and a 2" strip of coordinating fabric. Fold the fabric lengthwise and press. Insert the cording inside, fold over and use a zipper foot on the sewing machine to stitch close to the cording.

5 Round the corners of the pillow slightly to make sewing the piping on a little easier.

6 Place the pillow right side up and pin the cording in place. Baste close to the cording again.

7 Place the backing fabric and pillow top right sides together and stitch around all outside edges, leaving an opening large enough to allow you to turn the fabric right side out and insert the pillow form.

8 Turn the pillow right side out, insert the form and hand stitch the opening closed.

Stitched detail.

The fused image on "Winter Sky," made by Jan Wargo from Hope, New Jersey, nearly looks painted onto the background.

Finished size: 10" diameter

Crafters can use this Broderie Perse appliqué technique to embellish journals, boxes and scrapbooks with fabric motifs, as Yolanda has done with her textile notebook shown here.

Quilt artist Jennifer O'Brien used components cut from paper napkins (above) for fusing to create "Lavender in the Sun" (at right).

Finished size: 10" × 8"

Layered Rose Appliqué

Appliqué size: 7¼" × 8"

When you try this fused flower appliqué, not only will you be learning a valuable fusing technique, but you'll also be gaining insight into how textile designers think when they are rendering floral designs in a traditional style. Study how this rose is put together, and you are on your way to designing your own multi-layered appliqué blooms. Double-stick fusible web makes it a snap to reposition pieces over and over again until you are satisfied with your design.

Suggestion for a quilt that can be made incorporating the appliqué rose.

Materials

▶ **Fusing Supplies:**

(4) 8½" square sheets Steam-A-Seam 2 fusible web

▶ **Other Materials:**

(4) 8½" square sheets of 3 different colored fabrics: 1 dark, 1 medium and 2 light

▶ **Tools and Templates:**

Inkjet printer

Small, sharp scissors

8½" × 11" tracing paper

Transfer paper (Clover Chacopy™)

2 Teflon pressing sheets, at least 8½" × 11" (or 1 pressing sheet and 1 sheet of parchment paper)

Iron

2 bulldog clips or pins

Transparent or masking tape

Ballpoint pen

Templates from the CD: FusedRoseReversed, FusedRoseReversed1–4

Prepare the Rose Pieces

1 Print out the "FusedRoseReversed" templates 1–4.

2 Check to see which side the paper peels off easily on the SAS2. Trace the templates on each of the SAS2 squares on the side that does not peel off easily.

3 Peel off the looser side on all the SAS2 pieces and press to adhere to the back of each of your fabric squares.

4 With a hot iron, fuse the Fabric 1 pattern to the wrong side of the lightest fabric.

5 Fuse the Fabric 2 pattern to the wrong side of the medium fabric.

6 Fuse the Fabric 3 pattern to the wrong side of the darkest fabric.

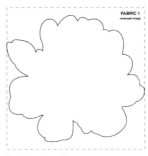

Fabric 1 pattern

Fabric 2 pattern

Fabric 3 pattern

Fabric 4 pattern

7 Fuse the Fabric 4 pattern to the wrong side of the other lightest fabric.

8 Cut out all the shapes, but do not peel off the second protective paper layer.

Make a Placement Guide

1 Print out the "FusedRoseReversed" template on tracing paper, or on regular paper and trace.

2 Apply tape across the top of the tracing paper to reinforce it while using it as a layout overlay.

3 Peel the protective paper from the base layer (Fabric 1) and place it on the pressing sheet.

4 Flip over the tracing paper image so it reads correctly and clip or pin it to the pressing sheet. Work on a hard surface where you can trace comfortably.

Bulldog clips hold the tracing in place over the fabric.

Build the Rose Layer by Layer

1 Position the Fabric 1 piece under the tracing so it aligns with the image on the tracing.

2 Insert the transfer paper, chalk side down, between the tracing and the background fabric. With a ballpoint pen transfer all the lines that correspond to Fabric 2. Refer to the printouts as a guide.

Transferring the Fabric 2 pattern lines onto the fabric.

3 Lift the tracing paper and transfer paper and position the Fabric 2 shape on top of Fabric 1. Hand press to adhere in position.

The second rose shape positioned over the first shape.

4 Flip the tracing and transfer papers back over the design and transfer all the lines for Fabric 3.

5 Position all Fabric 3 shapes on top and hand press.

6 Repeat this process with Fabric 4.

The third rose shape added.

The fourth rose shape added.

Finalize and Fuse the Layers

1 Now examine the multi-layered rose and make any changes before the final step of fusing the layers in place. The beauty of working with SAS2 is that it allows you to pick up the pieces and adjust as needed. The textured fusible layer has been engineered to be tacky so it will adhere with slight manual pressure before the final fusing is done with heat.

2 Once satisfied with the rose, take off the tracing layer and cover the rose with another protective pressing sheet (or parchment paper) and press until all the pieces are fused down.

3 When the rose cools, peel it off the pressing sheet as a unit and fuse it to any fabric, paper, canvas or wood where you want an appliqué-style rose. We chose to use our rose as the center of the quilt block shown on page 48.

"Tulip Trove 2004," a quilt made by Charlotte Warr Andersen, shows how layers can make up various blooms in the same piece. Incidentally, the twin of this quilt is used by Superior Threads at shows where they vend, to demonstrate how Charlotte's Fusible Web works—a fusible thread created by the company at Charlotte's request. (www.charlottewarrandersen.com)

Finished size: 17" × 23"

"Fairy Bride," from a pattern designed by Margo Rose (www.future-heirlooms.com), was made by Chris Campbell, a digital scrapbooker and new quilter from West Milford, New Jersey. She used a layering effect for the flowers surrounding her bride.

Finished size: 24" × 24"

Stencil-Style Lemon Tree Quilt

Finished size: 15" square

This lemon tree motif was inspired by a nineteenth-century Moses Eaton wall stencil in a house in New Hampshire. Wall stencils are a great source of fused appliqué ideas. There are many available that you can use to stencil walls and then make matching fabric projects. We'll add detail to this quilt using fusible ribbon.

Materials

▶ Fusing Supplies:

8½" × 11" piece of paper-backed fusible web

16" square fusible batting

4 packets of Hot Ribbon Art

Colors:

17 Honey (for lemons)

11 Lime Green (for stems)

9 Maroon and 13 Orange (for pot)

▶ Other Materials:

½ yd. medium red fabric; recut into (1) 18" square (for backing), (4) 2½" squares (for corners), (5) 2" × 22" strips (for binding), and selected pot pieces

14" × 14" square light taupe fabric (for background)

⅓ yd. green print, recut into (4) 2½" × 12½" pieces (for border)

6" × 6" scrap yellow fabric (for lemons)

8" × 6" scrap green fabric (for leaves)

3" × 6" scrap dark red fabric (for selected pot pieces)

▶ Tools and Templates:

Inkjet printer

Permanent and fabric markers

Rotary cutter and mat

Small, sharp scissors

Sturdy board or plywood

Masking tape

Painter's tape (optional)

11" × 14" tracing paper

Transfer paper (Clover Chacopy)

Ballpoint pen

Iron and mini-iron

Teflon pressing sheet

Basic sewing supplies

Templates from the CD: LemonTreeTop, LemonTreeBottom

Cut and Fuse the Patterns to Fabric

1 Print out the templates and tape them together. Label all twenty-nine pieces. Trace them onto the paper side of your fusible web, grouped by color family. Label all twenty-nine pieces. (If you are using Steam-A-Seam 2, first determine which paper side comes off more easily and trace on the other side.) They should all fit on the 8½" × 11" piece of fusible web.

Proposed layout of pattern pieces on the fusible web.

2 Cut the fusible web apart by grouping same-color shapes (for example, all leaves together). Remove the first paper backing and fuse down on the wrong side of the corresponding fabrics. Cut the web apart as needed to accommodate all pieces on the respective fabrics.

3 Attach the 14" × 14" background fabric to a sturdy, unwarped piece of board or plywood with masking tape. Mask the center 12" × 12" area with masking or painter's tape.

Pattern pieces fused onto fabric.

4 Trace the entire image on tracing paper, making sure to number all the pieces. Flip the tracing so it reads correctly. Verify against the photo of the finished piece. Position the tracing carefully in the center of the 14" × 14" background fabric. Tape or pin it across the top as a placement guide, so you can flip it up as needed.

Traced placement guide.

5 Using transfer paper, transfer the entire image to the fabric. A ballpoint pen works best for this.

6 Cut out all the pieces. Peel off the paper backing and fuse in place on the background fabric.

All fabric pieces in place.

Guide Your Lines

You can mark the stems with tiny dotted lines using a fabric marker to create a guide for adhering the fusible ribbon. Be sure to cover all the dots with the ribbon.

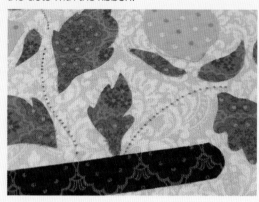

Apply Fusible Ribbon Details

1 Leave the background fabric taped to the board. This way it's easy to rotate the piece as you apply the ribbon.

2 Check that your mini-iron is clean. Preheat it to medium-high heat for at least five minutes. The ribbon will not adhere properly otherwise.

3 Start with the stems. Decide where the ribbon should begin to determine what angle would be best for the starting point of the ribbon, and snip accordingly.

4 Position the ribbon at the starting point and touch the tip of the mini-iron to that spot to anchor the ribbon. Wait long enough so that the adhesive on the ribbon melts and adheres the ribbon to the fabric.

Positioning the ribbon stems.

5 Let the ribbon flow naturally as you position and fuse each stem; don't pull on it. Turn the surface as you work, making it easier for the hands to work smoothly. You can reposition the ribbon while it's still warm; just lift off gently and fuse down again.

6 At the end of a stem, decide what would be the best angle for finishing, and snip carefully.

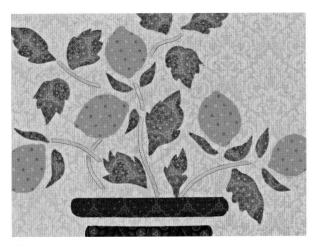

All stems fused in place.

Ribbon Tips

All ribbons in this project are applied in one continuous piece. Another project might call for a sharp curve or corner. In that case, cut the ribbon at an angle that matches the shape you want to outline. Overlap another piece of ribbon slightly over the previous piece, matching the angles of the cut to the shape of the outline.

Store unused ribbons in their original packaging to keep them in good condition and to have the name and color readily available. Save all the small pieces left over from a large project; they make wonderful confetti-style accents.

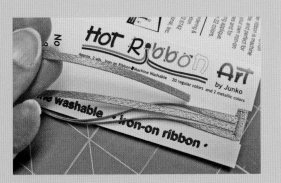

7 Outline all the lemons. Use the same technique, but with one new twist: overlap the ribbon over itself a bit at the end, as shown. Use the tip of the mini-iron to help guide the ribbon around tight curves.

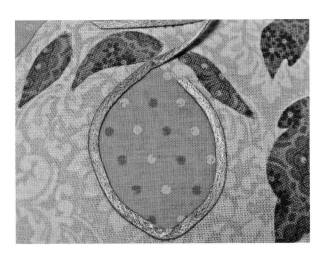

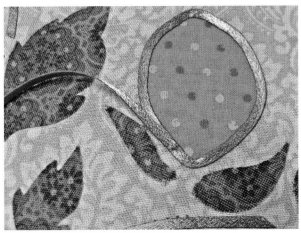

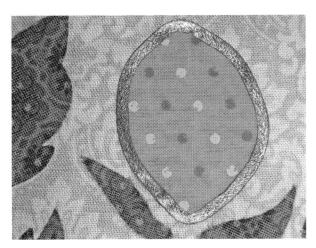

Applying ribbon around a curved piece.

8 Outline the pot using red ribbon around the medium red fabric and orange ribbon around the dark red fabric.

Easing the ribbon around the curves.

9 Once the ribbons are all fused, lay the pressing sheet over the entire design. Press with a hot iron to ensure the ribbons are well-attached.

Quilt center complete and ready to finish.

Add Borders

1 Trim the background square to 12½", centering the design.

2 Attach two green border strips to the sides of the quilt center, and press.

3 Sew two 2½" red squares onto the ends of each remaining border strip and attach these borders to the top and bottom of the quilt, then press.

Borders added.

Finish the Quilt

1 Layer the quilt top, fusible batting and backing and fuse in place or use the basting method of your choice.

2 We quilted around all the elements of the design and in the ditch around the borders.

3 Trim the quilt to 14½" square and bind with the red print, using your favorite method.

The finished quilt.

GALLERY

Fusible ribbon adds detail and drama to this quilt, "Radiant Fuschias," by Lennie Honcoop. At her website, you can learn more about Hot Ribbon Art classes and supplies. (www.dutchquilter.com)

Finished size: 35" × 36"

Decorative Ribbon Accents

You've not experienced true scrapbooking freedom until you've played with fabric and paper together using fusibles. For this project we consulted Barbara's three-year-old granddaughter, Sarah, a play expert sought frequently by many of her peers for playdates. Her advice? "Play with it all!" So this one is dedicated to Sarah, who is pictured on the scrapbook page below in one of her favorite play positions. Only fusibles were used to adhere everything onto the page. Rather than re-create the entire page, we'll list what we used for the purposes of inspiration, and focus on showing you how to braid fusible colored-fabric tape and use it to give unexpected texture to what otherwise might be a flat page.

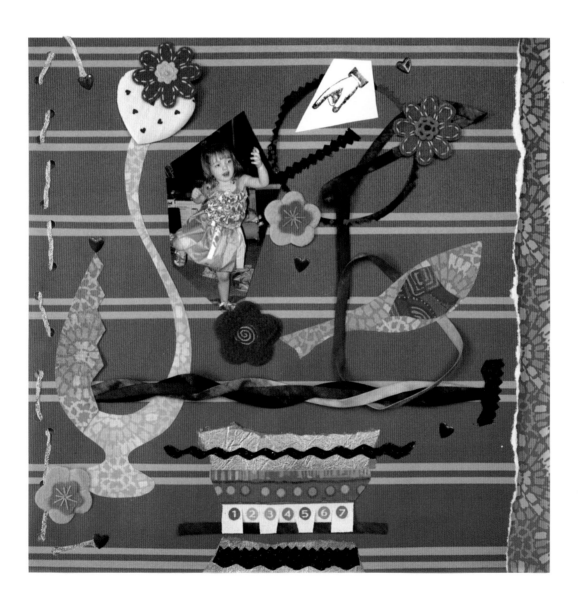

Materials

▶ Fusing Supplies:
  ¼" Clover Quick Bias fusible tape,
  11 yd. rainbow roll

▶ Other Materials:
  Mini-iron
  Teflon pressing sheet

▶ Other Fusing Supplies (for page):
  ¼" Steam-A-Seam 2 fusible tape
  Fusible web scraps
  Kreinik fusible decorative threads
  Iron-on heart nailheads (Kandi Corp.)

▶ Other Materials (for page):
  12" × 12" scrapbooking paper
  Various paper and fabric scraps (including
  selvedges), some with fusible web backing left
  over from other projects
  Assorted embellishments

Fuse a Braid

1 Cut three pieces of fusible bias tape all the
  same length (at least 12" so you can get a long
  enough braid, or longer if you wish).

2 Remove the paper backing and fuse the ends
  together on your pressing sheet, using the
  mini-iron.

3 Braid a few times and fuse again where they
  join, as shown. Continue braiding and fusing to
  make a braided strip of the desired length.

Fusing the ends of the ribbons together.

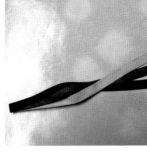

Braiding begins.   *Forming the braid.*

Fusing the ends of the ribbons together at intervals.

4 Carefully lift the braid off the pressing sheet and
  use it to embellish a scrapbook page or quilt
  by fusing it in place. The glue will still be good
  since it does not stick to the pressing sheet.

  Fusible bias tape can also be used freeform to
  create shapes and frame items on a page. We used
  it to form a loop for our fabric-scrap fish to jump
  through, and for one of our felt daisies to float
  on. Quilters love using it to create a stained-glass
  effect on quilts. Other fusible embellishments to
  try: weave fusible thread through holes punched
  in your paper, or apply fusible nailhead shapes.

Smooth Sailing

The best thing about fusing paper to paper,
fabric to paper or paper to fabric is that abso-
lutely no moisture is involved in the process.
There are no bumps, air bubbles or lumps to
deal with, even when fusing large pieces. You
gain a lot more control and create a permanent
bond, and your fingers don't get sticky in the
process.

Crystal Peacock Box

Finished size: 24" square

Yolanda found this interesting image on a nineteenth-century textile mill label. She thought the peacock's fanned-out tail provided a perfect opportunity to showcase fusible crystals. This embellished image creates a beautiful and very collectible box.

Materials

Fusing Supplies:

June Tailor Quick Fuse inkjet fabric sheet

Blue Zircon hot-fix Swarovski crystals, 2mm and 3mm (Kandi Corp.)

8 Brass It Up™ hot-fix metal copper wheels (Kandi Corp.)

Decorative crinkled gold metallic paper

2 pieces Steam-A-Seam 2 fusible web, at least 4½" × 6½"

Other Materials:

Unfinished, hinged wooden box: 4⅝" wide × 6⅝" long × 3½" tall, with a 4" × 6" recessed area in the lid (see "Finding a Box" sidebar on page 62)

Craft acrylic paint or spray paint of your choice

4" × 6" piece cardboard or book-binding board

Tools and Templates:

Inkjet printer (with color ink)

Teflon pressing sheet

Rotary cutter and mat

Iron and mini-iron
(protected with adhesive Teflon)

Kandi Kane hot-fix applicator

Fine or very fine sandpaper

Medium-size brush (if handpainting)

Tweezers

Dental pick (optional)

Artwork from the CD: Peacock

Prepare the Box

1 Lightly sand the box to prepare it for painting.

2 Paint the box with a spray or brush-on acrylic as desired. We painted everything blue except the inside of the lid and the inside of the bottom. The bottom inside was painted in a contrasting golden-honey tone.

The painted box.

3 Cut a piece of SAS2 and a piece of crinkled gold paper to the dimensions of the inside of the lid (4" × 6").

4 Peel off both protective papers on the SAS2 until all that remains is the fusible web. Lay it carefully in the inside of the lid, and place the gold paper on top of it. Fuse it with the Teflon-protected mini-iron.

Fusing gold paper to the inside of the lid.

The finished inside of the lid.

Decorate the Outer Lid

1 Using an inkjet printer, print the peacock image on an 8½" × 11" piece of Quick Fuse fabric sheet. (This image can also be printed on regular inkjet fabric and fused with Steam-A-Seam fusible web.)

2 Cut the image apart as shown, using a rotary cutter.

Cutting apart the printed peacock image.

Finding a Box

We found this box at a local craft store, but Walnut Hollow makes a similar one (Classic Box #3219) minus the recessed lid, which measures 5" x 6½" x 3" (see "Resources" on page 126). In lieu of the frame that a recessed lid provides, you can create a frame effect with fusible ribbon, fabric tape or thread. If the dimensions of your box differ slightly, be sure to factor that in as you work. Trim the pieces of the printed image, and the cardboard support, to fit your box.

3 Check to make sure that the 4" × 6" cardboard piece slips easily into the recessed area on the lid (or whatever your measurement is).

4 Place the cut-out center image of the peacock face down on the ironing surface. Center your cardboard on the image, and fold the image edges over on all four sides.

Back view of the cardboard-mounted center peacock piece.

5 Turn it over and fuse from the front side, using a pressing sheet with your iron.

6 Turn it over once again and apply a piece of SAS2 trimmed to the same size as the cardboard, with both protective papers removed.

7 Insert the card-mounted peacock image into the recessed lid area. Cover with the pressing sheet, and apply heat with your iron so that it fuses to the lid.

8 Cut out the side strip decorations, and fuse to the edges of the lid. Depending on your box style, you might need to remove hardware first to do this.

A side strip applied.

Embellish with Crystals and Copper

1 Pre-heat the hot-fix applicator for four minutes.

2 Place crystals onto the surface to be embellished using the tweezers. We used 2mm and 3mm crystals, placing the smaller ones on the inside of the peacock tail and graduating to larger ones on the outside.

Crystals on the peacock's tail are smallest near the body and larger around the outer edge.

3 Using the appropriate-size tip, place the hot-fix applicator on top of each crystal to melt the glue. Wait for the special adhesive on the back of the crystal to begin melting. This should take no more than ten to twelve seconds for most items. Then lift the applicator straight up. The crystal will stay attached to the surface. Note: If you want to change the tip to a different size, unplug the applicator and allow it to cool completely before removing the tip and replacing it with another. Do NOT touch any metal parts while the applicator is hot!

4 We used the flat tips (included in the Kandi Kane kit) to affix the eight copper wheels to the top of the box around the edges.

Applicator Cleaning Tips

The concave tips that come with the hot-fix applicator allow for better control, but the crystals can get stuck in the tip. A dental pick is useful for gently prying the crystals free. Or, simply use the flat tips instead, which can be used on any-size crystal.

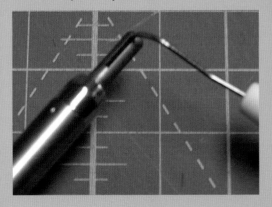

Kandi Corp. president Abby Riba embellished this denim jacket with crystals.

Holiday Cards

These homemade creations will stand out as special on anyone's mantel. We have barely skimmed the surface of what is possible with scraps of fabric and a bit of fusible embellishment. Enjoy making these fun greeting cards as much as the recipients will enjoy getting them.

Materials

▶ **Fusing Supplies:**

Bo-Nash bonding powder

Steam-A-Seam 2 fusible web

Kreinik Finishing Touches fusible iron-on threads (CB6-0004 CHRISTMAS packet)

Red Clover Quick Bias fusible tape

Fusible crystals and ribbon (optional)

▶ **Other Materials:**

7" × 10" cardstock, scored and folded in half

Lace vignette

Red and green fabric scraps

Envelope for 5" × 7" card

▶ **Tools:**

Mini-iron (protected with adhesive Teflon)

Water-filled spray bottle

Fuse Lace to Fabric or a Card

Because your card will depend on the lace motif you have, instead of giving detailed instructions to re-create this exact card, we'll explain how to fuse lace to fabric or directly to a card.

1 Sprinkle Bo-Nash bonding powder on a surface such as a sheet of paper or cardboard.

2 Spray the back of the lace vignette with water so it becomes slightly damp.

3 Press the lace wet-side down onto the powder. Pick it up and gently shake off the excess.

4 Lay the lace down carefully where you want it, powder-side down, and fuse using the Teflon-protected mini-iron.

5 Continue fusing scraps of fabric and fusible threads to the card to complement the lace motif.

"Lacy Holiday" card.

Materials

▶ Fusing Supplies:

Kreinik Finishing Touches fusible iron-on threads (CB6-0004 Christmas packet)

(2) 4" squares Steam-A-Seam 2 fusible web

▶ Other Materials:

4" square red fabric

4" square green fabric

(2) 7" × 10" pieces cardstock, scored and folded in half

2 envelopes for 5" × 7" cards

▶ Tools:

Iron and mini-iron (protected with adhesive Teflon)

Teflon pressing sheet

Pencil

Bulldog clips

Sharp, small scissors

Circle cutter (optional)

This project yields two cards.

Make the Ornaments

1 Peel off the looser paper side of the two SAS2 sheets. Press on the wrong side of each of the fabric pieces and fuse, using your iron.

2 Draw a 3¼" circle on the paper side of each fusible-backed fabric. Cut out the circles.

The basic ornament shapes.

3 Clip the two circles together with bulldog clips, aligning them one on top of the other, right sides up.

4 With small, sharp scissors, cut in a free-motion wave across the two circles twice, as shown.

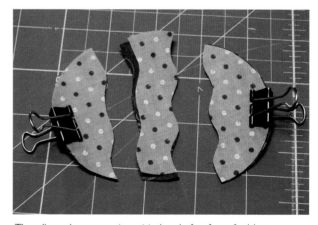

The clipped ornaments cut twice, in freeform fashion.

5　Mix up the pieces to get two red-and-green ornaments.

6　Peel off the remaining paper from the SAS2, and position as desired on two different cards. Fuse in place using your iron and a pressing sheet.

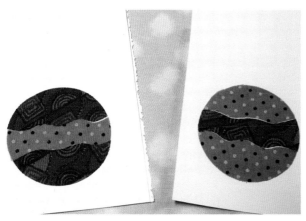

The ornaments fused on the cards.

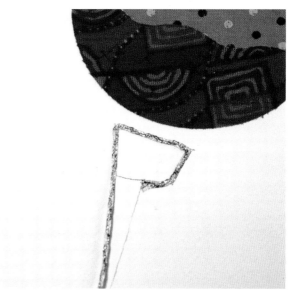

Embellish the Cards

1　Draw a top and string for each ornament lightly with the pencil, as shown.

2　Preheat the mini-iron for approximately four minutes at the highest setting to ensure a good fuse on the threads. Fuse the threads with the mini-iron, following the drawn line. Don't cut the thread off when you reach the top of the card.

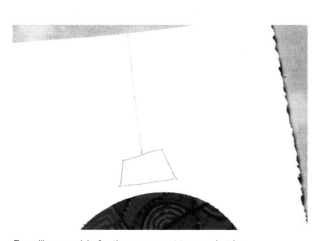

Penciling a guide for the ornament top and string.

Fusing the thread to the card.

3 Open the card, fold the thread over the edge and fuse down the string a length approximately 2½" long.

Folding the ornament string over to the inside.

4 Lightly sketch the word JOY, as shown.

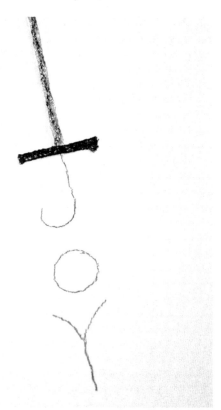

Penciling JOY where the string ends.

5 Finish off the words by fusing on the other threads from the Christmas pack.

Fusing on thread to form the letters.

6 Turn the card over to the front and add fusible red and green threads along the wavy edges of the ornament. Finish the second card in the same manner, changing the inside greeting, if you want.

Adding final threads to the ornament.

Materials

▶ **Fusing Supplies:**

Kreinik Finishing Touches fusible iron-on threads (CR8-0011 Blues and CIM-6020/20 I-O Silver packets)

Iron-on red heart nailhead (Kandi Corp.)

▶ **Other Materials:**

7" × 10" cardstock, scored and folded in half

Envelope for 5" × 7" card

▶ **Tools and Templates:**

Inkjet printer

Transfer paper

Ballpoint pen

Mini-iron (protected with adhesive Teflon)

Sharp, small scissors

Teflon pressing sheet

Templates from the CD: Peace

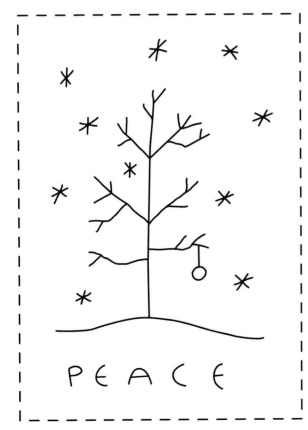

The "Peace" card template.

Create the Tree

1 Print out the template.

2 Transfer the image to the card front with the transfer paper and a ballpoint pen.

3 Preheat the mini-iron for about four minutes at its highest setting. The threads will not fuse down until the mini-iron has completely warmed up.

4 Unwind enough medium blue fusible thread (#6450 Royal Blue) to work with comfortably.

5 Snip off the end of the thread to get a nice, square starting point.

6 Using the transferred drawing as a guide, start to fuse at the base of the tree, holding the tip of the mini-iron on top of the thread until it adheres well.

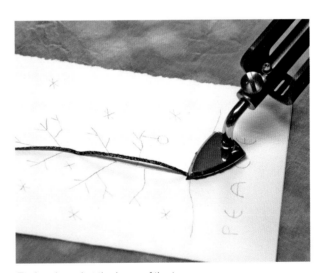

Fusing thread at the base of the tree.

Check it Out

Kreinik has an iron-on thread color chart on their website (www.kreinik.com). This comes in handy when planning new designs.

7 Carefully fuse all the way up the trunk, guiding the thread with your other hand. Be careful not to let the guiding fingers get too close to the tip of the mini-iron.

Fusing the tree trunk.

8 Snip off the thread where the trunk ends at a 45-degree angle so it looks more natural.

9 Add all the secondary branches, starting from the trunk out. Snip the starting points of the threads so that they match the angle where the thread meets the trunk.

Adding branches.

10 After fusing all the secondary branches, finish the tree by fusing all the missing smaller branches.

Filling in the smallest branches.

11 Add the snowline by fusing with the light blue thread (#6420 Sky Blue). Use this color again to make the hanger for the heart.

Adding a snow line and a hanger for the heart.

Add the Snowflakes, Message and Heart

1 Add all the snowflakes by fusing with the middle weight silver thread (#6020 Silver #16 braid).

2 Fuse the letters with the same thread used for the tree. Look closely at the following photos to see the easiest way to apply the threads to the letter shapes.

Snowflakes fused and the letters begun.

Finishing the letters.

3 Place the iron-on red heart in position, the pressing sheet over it, and fuse by holding the tip of the mini-iron on top of it. Be careful not to overheat. With the mini-iron fully heated, nailheads will set rather quickly on the cardstock because the metal transfers the heat very well.

A small piece of pressing sheet protects the finish of the metal heart during fusing.

Allow the heart to cool before touching.

More Fusing Fun

This section contains projects that explore further the uses of fusible products. Hone your fusing skills while creating some wonderful items for your home or to give as gifts.

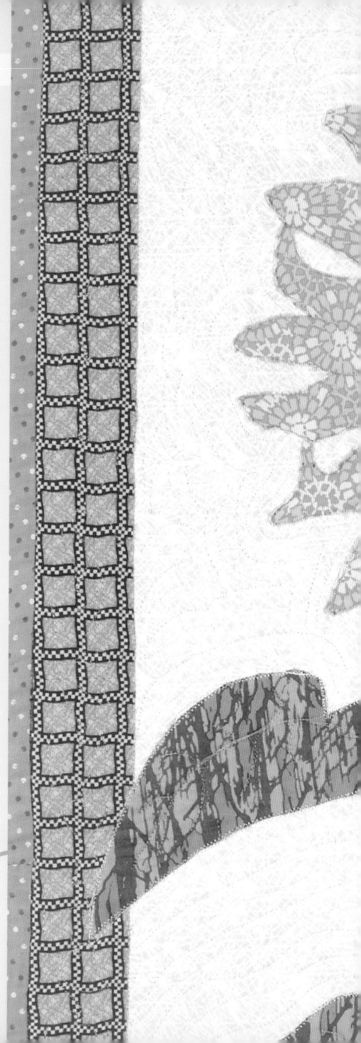

Freestyle Pumpkin Patch Quilt

Finished size: 20" × 22"

> *This seasonal quilt is a quick and easy project to make for decorating your home for autumn. It is the perfect size for a wall hanging or table mat; you can use the same leaf and pumpkin templates provided to make matching placemats and napkins. It also makes a fitting gift for your friends born during the season.*

Materials

▶ ## Fusing Supplies:

Steam-A-Seam 2 fusible web

22" × 24" fusible batting

▶ ## Other Materials:

Fat quarter red-orange (for pumpkins and leaves)

Fat eighth light orange (for pumpkins and leaves)

Fat eighth red (for apples and leaves)

Fat eighth gold (for leaves)

Dark green, light brown and mauve scraps (for stems and leaves)

Fat quarter taupe pattern print (for background)

⅔ yd. taupe stripe print (for bottom and left borders and backing)

¼ yd. dark brown (for binding)

Coordinating threads

MonoPoly invisible thread

▶ ## Tools and Templates:

Inkjet printer

Permanent marker

Rotary cutter and mat

Iron

Basic sewing supplies

Templates from the CD: PumpkinPatch1, PumpkinPatch2

Cut Your Fabric

1 Print out the templates.

2 Trace the pumpkins, apples, stems and leaves onto the paper side of the fusible web that does *not* lift as easily, allowing at least ½" between shapes. Refer to the templates and the finished quilt for suggestions on leaf shapes and colors. Trace at least four of each leaf shape to fuse to various colors. Trace one of each pumpkin shape and three apples.

3 Loosely cut out the shapes, leaving at least ¼" around each shape.

4 Fuse the web to the wrong side of fabrics chosen for the various shapes.

5 Cut out all shapes along the traced lines, and set them aside.

6 Trim the taupe background fabric to measure 18" × 20".

7 From the taupe stripe fabric, cut the backing to measure 23" × 25", then cut one 3¾" × 20" border and another 3¼" × 20¼".

8 Cut three 2" strips from the dark brown fabric and piece to measure at least 90" when sewn together for the binding.

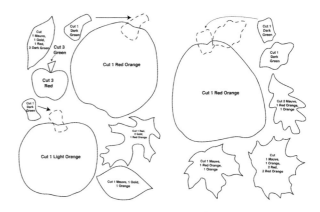

The quilt templates as they appear on the CD, with color suggestions.

Refer to this finished quilt when placing your pumpkins, fruit and leaves.

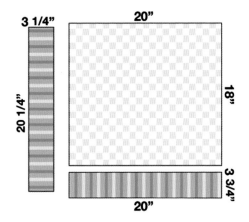

3 1/4" **20"**

20 1/4" **18"**

3 3/4"

20"

Sewing measurements and general layout.

Stitching and quilting details.

Assemble the Major Pieces

We assembled the quilt top with batting and backing before applying the leaf, apple and pumpkin shapes, as some of these shapes will overlap the border strips.

1 Sew one taupe stripe border strip to the bottom of the taupe background. Press, and trim the excess.

2 Sew the other taupe stripe border strip to the left side of the quilt top.

3 Layer the backing, fusible batting and quilt top and fuse the layers. (Or, use non-fusible batting with temporary spray adhesive or Bo-Nash bonding powder to hold the layers together.)

4 Trim the quilt top to measure 20" × 22". Machine baste around the borders and all outside edges to stabilize.

Machine Appliqué and Finish the Quilt

1 Remove the paper backing from the shapes. Referring to the photo of the finished quilt, arrange the pumpkins, apples, stems and leaves on the quilt top. Once satisfied with the placement, fuse in place. Reserve a few leaves to attach to the quilt after the binding is applied, if desired.

2 Stitch around the edges of all appliquéd pieces to secure them on the quilt, using MonoPoly invisible thread. You will be quilting while you are permanently affixing the pieces to the quilt top. We suggest stitching detail lines in the pumpkins and veins in the leaves.

3 Quilt the background after all the appliquéd pieces are quilted. The quilt pictured has swirling leaves quilted in the background with a coordinating cotton thread.

4 Attach the binding using your favorite method, then add some more leaves that reach the edge of the quilt in a few places, stitching them with invisible thread as you did with the previous leaves. (Refer to the finished quilt for suggested placement.)

5 Apply a hanging sleeve if desired.

About the Fabric

Fabrics used for the pumpkins and leaves in this project are from the Bold Over Batiks collection (www.boldoverbatiks.com). Bold Over Batiks is a partnership between Mary Scott, an American, and Faridah Abdul Rahman, a Malaysian. While working in Malaysia for a U.S.-based company, Mary was impressed by the beautiful batik fabrics created by this warm and easygoing people. Highly experienced batik artists painstakingly handcraft each piece using wax resists and dye.

A batik artist using a stamp to apply wax to fabric before dyeing it.

Hoping to keep this age-old craft alive in the local villages, Mary decided to sell these unique fabrics to the quilting community and joined forces with Faridah, who began as Mary's interpreter but has since joined her as a partner. The pair deal only with family-based businesses, where a piece of art is passed around the entire village to execute the manual processes. They remain committed to keeping this batik cottage industry alive and helping to support these devoted artists and their communities. Because of their efforts, the craftspeople are paid fairly for their work.

GALLERY

Fusing can ease the process of putting together freestyle quilts like this one—a double-sided mobile called "Before/After" by Pennsylvania artist Cathy Neri. (www.cathyneriquilts.com)

Finished size: 11" diameter

No-Sew Games-to-Go Table Mat

Finished size: 38" square

Having raised two boys and now entertaining grandchildren, Barbara has always appreciated old-fashioned game boards. She no longer has a playroom and needs something that can easily be stored. This game mat is designed to fit a standard folding card table. Fuse everything in place and watch the fun begin! If you decide this mat needs additional stability, you can stitch down all the intersections with a zigzag stitch and invisible thread. Except for the card motifs, it's all straight, simple sewing.

Materials

▶ **Fusing Supplies:**

Pellon fusible quilter's grid (with 1" squares)

Wonder-Under or other lightweight, paper-backed fusible web

4 yd. square Steam-A-Seam fusible web (for attaching the mat backing)

Bo-Nash bonding powder (optional)

▶ **Other Materials:**

½ yd. light blue felt

Precut piece (9" × 12") red felt

¼ yd. or 6 precut pieces white felt

⅓ yd. black felt

1¼ yd. backing fabric

Optional: ¼ yd. binding fabric, monofilament invisible thread, coordinating black and red threads

▶ **Tools and Templates:**

Inkjet printer

Rotary cutter and mat

Ruler

Sharp scissors

Iron

Basic sewing supplies (optional)

Templates from the CD: Cards

Cut the Fabric

1 Print out the template, which contains patterns for the playing card motifs.

2 Trace each shape onto the paper side of the Wonder-Under or other lightweight fusible web, and cut out loosely.

3 Fuse the shapes to the wrong side of the appropriate felt colors (black for the club and spade, red for the heart and diamond).

4 Cut out the shapes with sharp scissors on the drawn lines and set aside.

5 Cut the other components.

From the backing fabric:

(1) 40" square

From the black felt:

(2) 2" × 36" strips and
(2) 2" × 38" strips (borders)

(32) 1½" squares (checkerboard)

From the light blue felt:

(4) 12" squares and (4) 6" squares

(32) 1½" squares (checkerboard)

From the white felt:

(12) 6" squares

Table Tips

Most folding card tables are 37", 38" or 40". This project measures 38" when finished. For a smaller table, eliminate the border strip. If the table is larger, then increase the size of the border to fit.

Our fabric requirements are based on craft felt (100-percent polyester and washable), which we found sold in 72" widths. Wool felt (35-percent wool, 65-percent rayon) is also available in 36" widths; it is more durable, but must be dry-cleaned. If using wool felt, adjust the yardage accordingly.

Fuse the Pieces Together

1 Fuse the playing card motifs on four white squares as shown. Stitch in place to secure with a buttonhole or zigzag stitch and coordinating or contrasting thread, if desired.

The playing card motifs fused and stitched.

2 Cut and piece the fusible grid to measure at least 2" larger than on all sides than the finished size of your game table mat, including borders. We used Pellon's quilter's grid for our piece cut 42" long from the bolt, which measured 42" wide.

3 Position the 6" and 12" blue and white squares, following the layout diagram. Fuse in place.

The blue and white squares fused on the fusible grid.

4 Position the 1½" black and blue squares for the checkerboard in the center. Fuse in place.

5 Fuse the border strips in place.

6 After everything was fused in place on the front side, we turned the entire game mat over and pressed with our iron to make sure all the glue on the grid was melted and there was a good adhesion to the felt before adding the backing.

The checkerboard and border strips in place.

Finish the Mat

If you decide this is to be a no-sew project, fuse Steam-A-Seam to the back of the table mat and then fuse on a 40" square of backing fabric. Trim the table mat from the front to square it up to the desired size to fit your table.

We found that using the Pellon grid and the Steam-A-Seam fusible web made our table mat durable enough for our needs. If you decide to sew a zigzag stitch between squares to the background grid to secure for folding and storing, use invisible monofilament thread.

The finished game table mat, backed with fun themed fabric.

1 Fuse the fabric (or felt) backing to the front, using Steam-A-Seam fusible web or Bo-Nash bonding powder.

2 Put invisible thread in your sewing machine and set to a medium zigzag stitch.

3 Follow all straight lines where the squares come together to stitch the felt pieces to the background.

4 Stitch where the borders join the game mat and around all edges to securely join the front and back sides.

5 If you choose, you can bind this project as you would a regular quilt, using four strips of 2" fabric binding.

6 Make your checkers from felt and cardboard, if desired, or use plastic ones from an existing checker set.

Why just sit around and wait for Grandma to finish the game table mat when we can fuse, too? Barbara's grandchildren show off their own designs: a spaceship battle by Scott, age 11, and a celestial scene by Caitlyn, age 9. When fusing with children, be sure to supervise their use of the hot irons and make certain they understand how important it is to be careful.

Sunflower Door Banner

Finished size: 47" × 23"

This quilted banner incorporates "donut"-style appliqué, which we first saw on page 23.
This method uses the fusible web only on the outside edges of the pieces (hence the donut).
It makes the appliqué stable enough for machine stitching, but allows for a softer, more
flexible finished piece. With a tape measure added to the side border of this banner, it
would make a fabulous growth chart for your little ones.

Materials

▶ **Fusing Supplies:**

½ yd. 18" wide Steam-A-Seam 2 fusible web

▶ **Other Materials:**

(*Note:* Fabrics used in this quilt are from the Software line designed by Yolanda.)

Fat eighth Pink Dots

Fat quarter Orange Blossoms

Fat quarter Green Trees

⅛ yd. Pink Blossoms

⅙ yd. Orange Trees

⅙ yd. Pink/Yellow Stripes

½ yd. Orange Check

½ yd. Green Dots

⅝ yd. Yellow Grass

24½" × 48½" piece backing fabric

24½" × 48½" piece batting (reserve leftover for cutting Piece 16 flaps)

Coordinating threads (for piecing, machine appliqué and quilting)

▶ **Tools and Templates:**

Inkjet printer

Rotary cutter and mat

Permanent marker

Iron

Basic sewing supplies

Templates from the CD: Sunflower A–H, Sunflower Flap

Cut the Strips and Background

Cut the following strips from each fabric.

Pink Blossoms: (2) 1½" × 21½"

Orange Trees: (2) 3½" × 21½"

Pink/Yellow Stripes: (2) 2½" × 21½"

Orange Check: (2) 2½" × 32½"

Green Dots: (2) 2½" × 24" and (2) 1½" × 44½"

Plus, cut this piece for the background:

Yellow Grass: 17½" × 31½"

Sew the Background and Plan for the Borders

1 Sew the two orange check strips to the yellow background (see quilt layout diagram).

2 Sew one pink/yellow strip to one pink blossom strip. Attach a orange tree strip to the other side of the pink blossom. Repeat to make a duplicate border strip. Reserve these border strips until the appliqué is fused in place.

3 When you have finished the appliqué placement and stitching (instructions on page 84), add the top and bottom border sets to the quilt top, referring to the diagram.

Quilt layout diagram

4   Sew the green dot borders to the sides of the quilt, and finally the green dot strips to the top and bottom (again, refer to the diagram).

Complete the Donut-Style Appliqué

1   Print out the pattern templates.

2   Trace the patterns onto the paper side of the SAS2 that doesn't peel off as easily. Loosely cut out the pattern pieces, leaving at least ¼" from the outside of the drawn lines. Cut each larger piece about ¼" inside the drawn line. Do not cut inside the smaller stems; just use the entire pattern to fuse to the back of that fabric.

3   Fuse the pattern pieces to the wrong side of the appropriate fabrics, as follows:

   Pieces 1–6 (for the leaves): fat quarter green trees

   Pieces 7–13 (for stems): green dot print

   Piece 14 (for flower center): pink dot print

   Piece 15 (for sunflower): orange blossom print

   (5) Piece 16 (for flaps): green dot print

   (5) Piece 16 (for flaps): backing fabric

4   Cut out all pattern pieces on the drawn line.

5   Lay all pieces onto the quilt background. When satisfied with the arrangement, fuse in place, following the manufacturer's instructions.

6   Use a zigzag or buttonhole to stitch around all the leaf and stem appliqué pieces using a coordinating green thread. You will stitch the flower down during the quilting process.

7   Assemble the flap pieces by sewing the green dot and background pieces, right sides together around the curved edges. Leave the top edge open. Turn the piece right side out and press.

8   Pin the flaps to the bottom edge of the quilt as shown, leaving ½" from each edge open. They will overlap slightly. Machine baste in place.

The flaps pinned in place.

Quilt and Finish

1   Return to page 83 and follow the instructions for attaching the borders post-appliqué.

2   Layer the quilt top right side up (with the flaps to the inside), the backing wrong side up and the batting and baste the layers, lining up the edges on all pieces.

3   Sew around the outside edges with a ¼" seam, making sure that the flaps stay inside the sandwich. Leave a 5"—6" opening on one side so you can turn the quilt right side out.

4   Turn the quilt right side out and hand stitch the opening closed.

5   Press the quilt and top stitch around all the edges to keep them from turning.

6   Quilt in the ditch around all the borders to stabilize the quilt top. Use a free-motion stitch and a coordinating thread to stitch around all the outside edges of the sunflower and pink center. Quilt the background as desired. For a puffy sunflower center, slit open the back of the quilt behind the center and stuff it with a little polyester filling. Hand stitch the opening closed.

7   Add a hanging sleeve and a label, if desired.

Sunflower Tote

Finished size: 17" × 21"

> Designed to match the sunflower banner, the pattern on this tote is applied using the regular fusible appliqué method instead of the "donut-style" technique used for the banner. The pattern pieces are the same, just on a smaller scale. The tote itself is large enough for a trip to the beach, a shopping excursion or for packing a picnic.

Materials

▶ Fusing Supplies:
1 yd. Steam-A-Seam 2 fusible web

2 pieces 1¾" × 40" non-woven fusible interfacing (for handles)

▶ Other Materials:
(*Note:* Fabrics used in this bag are from the Software line designed by Yolanda.)

1¼ yd. Orange Dots

⅞ yd. Yellow Tonal

⅛ yd. Orange Check

⅓ yd. Purple Tonal

Fat quarter green print
(for cutting leaves and stems)

⅝ yd. muslin, recut into (2) 20" × 23" pieces (for backing on quilted pieces)

(2) 20" × 23" pieces Warm & Natural batting

Coordinating threads (for piecing and quilting)

Coordinating threads (for piecing, machine appliqué and quilting)

▶ Tools and Templates:
Inkjet printer

Permanent marker

Tape

Rotary cutter and mat

Iron

Basic sewing supplies

Templates from the CD: ToteA, ToteB

For Napkins

Download free instructions for making coordinating reversible napkins at www.loveinstitches.com.

Cut the Fabrics

Cut the following from each fabric.

Orange Dots:

(2) 18½" × 21½" pieces (for lining)

(2) 4" × 40" pieces (for straps)

Piece B (flower center)

Purple Tonal:

(2) 4½" × 21½" strips (for top borders)

Piece A (flower)

Yellow Tonal:

14½" × 17½" piece (for main body)

Orange Check:

2½" × 14½" strips (for side borders)

Sew on Borders and Prepare the Pattern

1 Sew a side border strip to either side of the yellow tote bag front. Repeat for the back piece.

2 Sew a purple tonal top border onto each of the tote bag sides.

3 Print the pattern templates.

4 Tape together and trace these patterns onto the paper side of the fusible web, leaving at least ½" of space between pattern pieces. Patterns have been reversed for this machine appliqué method. Cut apart loosely.

5 Fuse the web to the wrong side of the appropriate fabrics. Cut out each piece carefully along the drawn line.

6 Fuse the sunflower, stem and leaves to the front of the tote bag, using the layout as a reference.

Layout of tote bag front, with flower patterns in place.

Quilt the Bag

1 Layer and baste the muslin and the tote front to one piece of the batting and stitch around the edge of all appliquéd pieces to secure, using free-motion and coordinating threads.

2 Refer to the photo of the finished bag for quilting suggestions. We echo-quilted around all the appliqué pieces. A meandering leaf pattern was quilted in the borders.

3 Repeat the layering and quilting process for the back of the tote. This piece was quilted with a meandering flower and leaf pattern.

4 If desired, attach a pocket to the lining piece before assembling the tote. Make a large divided pocket for storing your picnic flatware and another large pocket for holding napkins or other picnic goodies. Sew these pockets to the lining pieces before they are sewn together.

Assemble and Finish the Bag

1 Sew the tote front and back, right sides together around the sides and bottom.

2 Sew the lining pieces together along both sides and bottom, leaving a 6"–7" opening to turn.

3 To create the bottom slanted corners, keep right sides together and mark a diagonal line 4" from the bottom and side on the corners of both bag and lining. Stitch along that line. Trim excess fabric from this seam to reduce bulk.

4 Turn the bag right side out and position the lining right side facing the outside of the bag. Pin carefully along the top edge and stitch the top seam.

5 Turn the lining to the inside of the tote bag and hand-stitch the opening.

6 Top stitch along the top edge, leaving about a ½" of lining showing on the outside of the bag as shown, to create the look of a binding.

7 Fold ¼" along one long edge of the 4" × 40" handle strips and press. Fold both ends into the center and press, overlapping the folded edge over the raw edge. Open these strips and insert the fusible interfacing. Re-fold and press with the iron to secure. Use a zigzag or decorative stitch to sew along the length to permanently secure the edges.

8 Fold the bottom of the straps in 1" and pin to the inside of the front of the tote, along the seam between the yellow and purple border. Stitch securely. Stitch again on the seam between the purple and orange "binding" piece. Repeat to attach the handle to the other side of the front. Repeat to attach the other handle to the back of the tote.

Double-Cute Fabric Frame

On a recent trip to New Zealand, Yolanda met this adorable little
boy who is the grandson of Penny Zino, designer of Flaxmere
Garden, a jewel of a country garden on the South Island.
Yolanda spent a lovely afternoon exploring the garden and came
away with much inspiration and some great photos. The two
photos of the boy, though, were the best, and only a custom-made
frame could properly do justice to his charm. It would also make
a perfect gift for his grandmother, a one-of-a-kind thank-you for a
memorable day spent in an amazing place.

View of a pool at Flaxmere, Penny
Zino's masterpiece garden.

The double frame when closed.

Materials

▶ **Fusing Supplies:**

3 yd. 12" wide Steam-A-Seam 2 fusible web

2 yd. ¼" Steam-A-Seam 2 fusible tape

▶ **Other Materials:**

13" × 19" sheet book-binding board, at least 80 pt. thick

2 precut 8" × 10" mats with 5" × 7" openings

19" × 12¼" fabric (for outside cover)

16¾" × 10" fabric (for inside cover lining)

(2) 10" × 12" pieces coordinating fabric (to cover mats)

Acid-free photo document tape or similar adhesive tape

8 small squares industrial-strength Velcro

▶ **Tools:**

Pencil

Quilter's grid ruler

Utility knife

Cork-backed metal ruler (18" or 24")

Iron

Teflon pressing sheet

Rotary cutter and mat

Glue gun (optional)

Make the Hinged Cover

1 Cut the board to measure 17" wide by 10¼" high.

2 Mark two lines at 8⅛" parallel to the short sides. This creates a center area which is ¾" wide and becomes the spine of the folding frame. (We've used marker instead of pencil for instructional purposes only; be sure to use pencil, especially when planning to cover with light-colored fabrics, which markers might show through.)

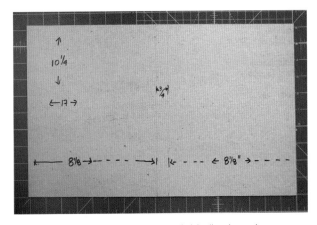

Marked measurements on the book-binding board.

Buy Book-Binding Board

You might be tempted to substitute mat board or illustration board for the book-binding board, but eventually these will warp from the moisture in the air. If you're going to go through the trouble of making a special frame, use the traditional book-binder's board that has been formulated not to warp. Dense and sturdy, it is best cut by hand with a very sharp utility knife, using a cork-backed metal ruler as a guide and gradually going into the cut several times until you cut all the way through. It can be purchased in bulk or by the 13" × 19" sheet and comes in at least four thicknesses (see "Resources" on page 126).

3 Carefully cut halfway through the board at the lines just marked. This will create the hinges by leaving some of the board uncut. The side of the board that has the "hinges" (the side not cut through) becomes the outside of the frame.

Cutting halfway through the board to make the hinges.

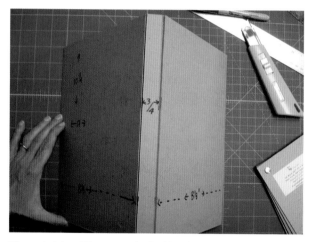

The cut side will become the inside of the folding frame.

4 Lay the board flat, hinge side (or outside) up.

5 Cut a piece of SAS2 exactly the same size as board. Use the board as a template. Strip off the looser paper side of the SAS2 and match it up to the hinge side of the board. Press it down well so it stays, then fuse it with a hot iron.

6 Take the 19" × 12¼" piece of fabric of your choice for the outside of the double frame and place it on a flat, even surface wrong-side up.

7 Peel the second piece of paper from the SAS2 that's fused to the board to expose the fusible web. Center the board sticky-side down on the fabric. You will have an inch of the fabric showing all around the board.

The board centered on the frame's back fabric.

8 Press the board down so that the fabric adheres to it. Pick up the board with the fabric and carefully turn it over. Fuse the fabric to the board.

9 Cut two pieces of SAS2 tape measuring 17". Position one each along the top and the bottom edges of the board. Press down well and remove the release paper. Fold the fabric over the edges and press to fuse.

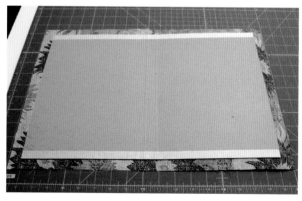

Tape in place, ready for fabric to be folded over and fused.

10 Fold and finger-press all the corners as shown.

11 Cut a 10¼" piece of the SAS2 tape and position it along the edge of the fabric over the folded corners. Trim the ends of the tape carefully after placing it.

A folded-back corner, before the tape is applied.

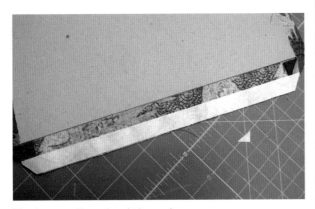

The tape positioned and trimmed.

12 Take the 16¾" × 10" piece of fabric for the inside cover and place it wrong-side down on a 17" × 10¼" piece of SAS2 with the protective paper peeled off on one side. Hand press so it adheres to the fabric, and trim off any excess SAS2. Fuse it to the fabric with the paper still attached to the other side.

13 Once fused, remove the second protective paper and place the fabric down on the inside of the cover. Fuse the fabric to the board.

Fusing the fabric to the inside cover.

Cover the Precut Mats

1 Take the first piece of 10" × 12" fabric. Place it wrong-side down on a piece of SAS2 that measures at least 10¼" × 12¼" and has had the protective paper peeled off of one side. Hand press so it adheres to the fabric, and trim off any excess SAS2. Fuse to the fabric with paper still attached to the other side.

2 Once fused, peel off the second protective paper and lay the precut mat face down and centered on the fusible side of the fabric. Press lightly so that the SAS2 adheres temporarily.

Fusing fabric to a precut mat.

3 While the mat and fabric are still face down, mark an opening in the fabric 1" smaller than the precut mat opening an all sides. Use a rotary cutter to cut out this inside rectangle.

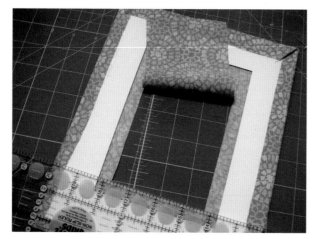

Making a picture opening in the fabric.

4 Make diagonal cuts in all four inside corners as shown.

Diagonal cuts in the inside corners.

5 Fold over all the fabric edges and fuse to the mats as shown in the diagrams and photo.

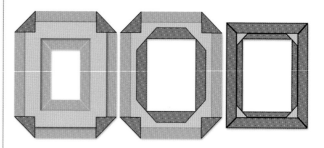

How the edges should fold.

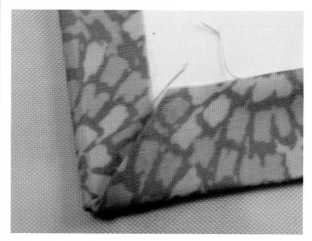

Edges fused in place.

Frame Your Photos

1 Affix photos in the windows with acid-free photo document tape.

2 To mount the mats to the hinged cover, place four squares of industrial-strength Velcro on the corners of each mat and press into place. This lets you replace the photos, should you ever want to. Or, glue permanently if you wish.

Fabric-Covered Tissue Box

If you're like us, you enjoy having things in your work area that have meaning beyond their functional value. Take this opportunity to showcase some lovely piece of fabric you've been hoarding away by adding some personality to a wooden tissue box.

Materials

▶ **Fusing Supplies:**

Steam-A-Seam 2 fusible web: 7" × 24" for sides
of box, 9" square for box top

Clover Quick Bias fusible tape in a
coordinating color

▶ **Other Materials:**

(*Note:* The fabric used is from the Chelsea
Morning line designed by Yolanda.)

7" × 24" fabric for sides of box

9" square coordinating fabric for top of box

Walnut Hollow Boutique Tissue Box
(#1136OP)

▶ **Tools:**

Permanent marker

Iron and mini-iron with half-ball attachment
(we used the Clover Mini Iron II)

Teflon pressing sheet

Tape measure

Scissors

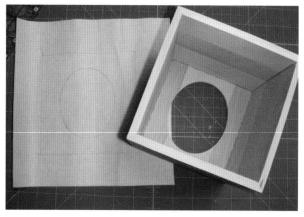

The top of the box traced onto paper-backed fusible web.

Second set of lines drawn.

Prepare the Box Top

1 Trace the top of the wooden tissue box onto
the paper side of the SAS2 that does not peel
off easily.

2 Draw a line 1½" from all around the outside
square and an inner oval about 1½" in from the
center oval. Fuse onto the wrong side of the
box top fabric.

3 Trim the fusible-backed fabric to the outside
square. Cut away the smaller oval. Snip the
center all around to just short of the larger oval.

Cutting the smaller oval and connecting tab lines.

Fuse Fabric to the Box Top

1 Peel away the second paper backing and center the top of the tissue box down on the SAS2 side as shown. Press down so it adheres in position.

The fabric centered on the box top.

2 Turn over and fuse the fabric to the top of box, using the pressing sheet.

3 Fold over the outside edges all around the box as shown, then fuse them down.

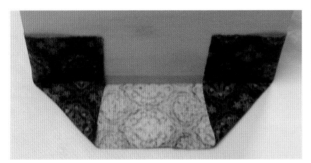

The top of the box will look like this.

4 Snip the tabs in half that were previously cut, and fuse them down to the inside edge of the oval with the mini-iron using the half-ball attachment.

Fusing the tabs along the inside edge.

5 Turn the box over and finish fusing the tabs to the inside of the box.

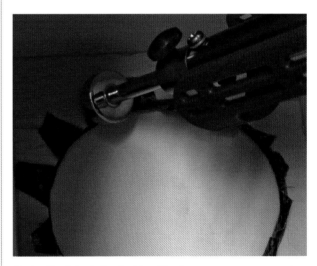

Fusing the tabs to the inside of the box.

6 Measure the circumference of the oval opening with the tape measure. Cut a piece of fusible bias tape ½" longer than the circumference. Apply the tape with the mini-iron all around the inside perimeter of the oval. Overlap the ends about ¼" and snip. Go around with the mini-iron once more to secure it well.

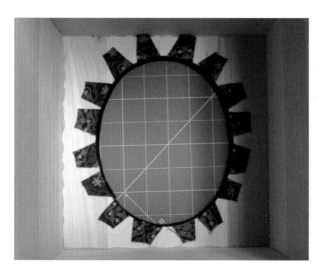

The inside edge of the oval finished with fusible bias tape.

View from the inside.

Finish the Box Sides

1 Measure the circumference of the box and add 2".

The circumference of this box measures 22".

2 Measure the height of the box and add ¾".

The height of this box is about 6¼".

3 Draw a rectangle the size of the padded measurements (7" tall × 24" around for our box) onto the paper side of the SAS2 that does not peel off as easily.

4 Fuse this to the back of the fabric you have chosen for the sides.

5 Cut the fusible-backed fabric to the size of the rectangle you have drawn.

6 Peel off the paper backing and begin to wrap the fabric around the box. When the fabrics meet, tuck the end under the first piece and pat it down.

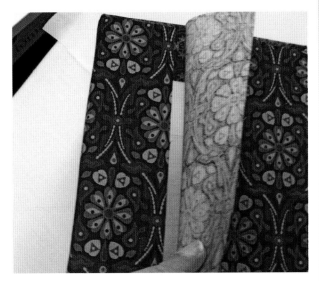

Tucking the excess under the starting point.

7 Check to make sure everything is in position and all is flat. When satisfied, fuse the fabric to the sides of the box, using the pressing sheet.

Fusing the fabric onto the sides.

8 Turn the box upside down and fuse the edges over to the bottom edge.

The edges fused over the bottom.

9 Finish the box by folding the remaining fabric inside and fusing with the mini-iron and half-ball attachment.

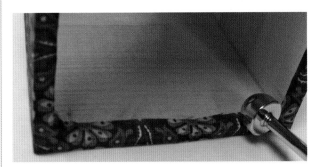

Fusing the excess to the inside of the box.

GALLERY

Once Yolanda made the tissue box, the idea of a matching letter tray was not far behind. The set makes a really special but simple-to-make gift.

Stylish No-Sew Belt and Headband

Accessorize your wardrobe! Using simple fusing techniques, you can make belts and headbands to coordinate with any outfit. Whether you are looking for an accessory to create for yourself or for someone else, both items are fabulous to wear and easy to make. They are perfect for all ages, especially children and teens. Crystals add an extra bit of glitz. These accessories were designed and made by guest artist Nina Kolpin, who was gracious enough to also model them for us.

Materials

▶ **Fusing Supplies:**

    5 yd. ¼" fusible tape

    Heavy fusible interfacing (glue on one side)

    Fusible Swarovski crystals (optional)

▶ **Other Materials:**

    (*Note:* The fabric used is from the Chelsea Morning line designed by Yolanda.)

    ⅛ yd. fabric of your choice

    1 yd. 1½" grosgrain ribbon (for belt)

    ½ yd. ¾" grosgrain ribbon (for headband)

    1½–2 yd. ⅝" satin ribbon (to coordinate)

    Plastic headband (available in craft shops)

    Rhinestone or other decorative buckle (optional)

    Fabric glue (optional)

▶ **Tools and Templates:**

    Pen or pencil

    Rotary cutter and mat, or scissors

    Iron or mini-iron

    Crystal applicator tool (optional)

Belt Instructions

1 Measure the waist for the desired length of belt. This style of belt can be worn around the waist or lower around the hips. Measurements do not have to be exact, as the satin ribbon will allow some adjustment to the desired size.

2 Determine the width of the belt. If using a buckle, the width of the belt will be pre-determined by the size of the buckle. The finished size of this belt is approximately 2". The ends of the belt were tapered down to about 1".

3 Draw a pattern for the belt on the interfacing with a pencil or pen, and cut it out on the drawn lines.

4 Fuse the wrong side of the fabric to the glue side of the interfacing, centering it on any fabric motif, if desired. Use the interfacing as a guideline to trim the fabric. Leave at least a ½" of fabric extending around the all the edges. For the belt shown, the fabric measured approximately 3" × 33", tapered at the ends to approximately 2".

5 Cut two lengths of fusible tape the same measurement as the length of the belt and fuse to the raw edges of the fabric. Fuse the fabric to the back of the belt. Cut two more lengths for the ends of the belt and then fuse the ends down.

6 Cut two pieces of satin ribbon to the desired lengths for the ties plus 4" and place on the ends of the belt, extending in at least 3". Use fusible tape to hold this in place for the next step. *Note:* It is advisable to cut the ribbon longer than you will need, as you can trim to the correct length once the project is complete.

7 Measure the back of the belt and cut the 1½" grosgrain ribbon to this length. Cut two strips of the ¼" fusible tape, and press to the wrong side of the edges of the grosgrain ribbon.

8 Center the grosgrain ribbon on the back of the belt, covering the raw edges of the fabric, satin ribbon and the interfacing and fuse in place. Trim the sides of grosgrain by tapering the edges. If the grosgrain ribbon appears to fray, use a light coating of fabric glue to reduce fraying.

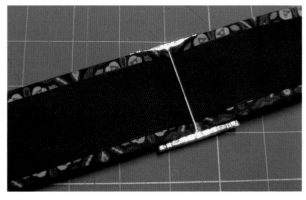

Back of belt.

9 Slide the rhinestone buckle into place and center accordingly. You may choose to embellish the fabric area within the buckle using fusible crystals.

Rhinestone buckle added.

10 If desired, use fusible Swarovski crystals to further embellish the belt, depending on the fabric design.

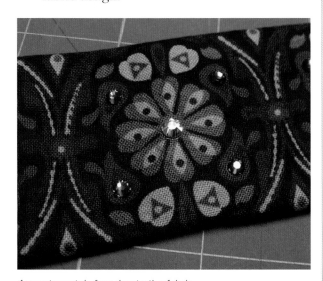

Accent crystals fused onto the fabric.

Another accessory made easily with fusing: this evening purse, created by needle artist Jacqui Clarkson from Rockaway, New Jersey, and Halliburton, Canada.

Headband Instructions

1 Choose a plastic headband to use for the basic structure (any width). Measure the length and width of your headband to create a template. (The one we used measures 1¾", which is the widest portion in the middle, and tapers down to ½".)

2 Draw the template on the back of the fabric and cut out the pattern.

3 Place strips of fusible tape onto the outer portion of the headband and iron gently. Repeat the same step for the inner portion of headband. Tuck in the ends of the fabric and fuse, easing and gently tucking to fit.

4 Use a piece of grosgrain ribbon for the inner side of headband, therefore hiding any imperfections. Fuse the grosgrain ribbon in place using ¼" fusible tape.

5 Embellish the headband with fusible Swarovski crystals, if desired.

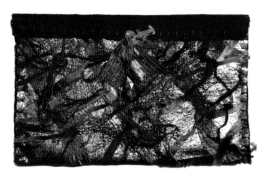

Fuse-by-Number Wall Art

Finished size: 24" × 18" × 2½"

When Yolanda was 7, she and her parents immigrated to New York City from Cuba, where they were received with open arms by her aunt's generous family, who had been living in the U.S. since the early 1950s. To commemorate their arrival, a photo of the family was taken in front of a paint-by-number vase of roses that Yolanda's cousin Myriam had painted. Yolanda was fascinated by the picture, never having seen anything like it. To this day, every time she sees any paint-by-number piece, she recalls with much love and gratitude the family and the city that took her in. The picture that influenced her to become both a fine artist and textile designer is the inspiration for this fuse-by-number version.

Yolanda and her parents in front of the inspiration painting.

Materials

▶ ## Fusing Supplies:

3 yd. Steam-A-Seam 2 fusible web

Kreinik Finishing Touches fusible iron-on threads (1 spool or card of your choice)

▶ ## Other Materials:

24" × 18" × 2½" deep-edge gallery-style canvas (staples on back), available at craft and art supply stores

Fabric (see chart at right and "Choosing Fabric" on page 103)

▶ ## Tools and Templates:

Inkjet printer

Permanent marker

Tape

Rotary cutter and mat

Scissors

Tape measure

Iron and mini-iron (protected with adhesive Teflon)

Teflon pressing sheet

Tracing paper

Masking or painter's tape

Transfer paper (Clover Chacopy)

Ballpoint pen

Templates from the CD: A_CeilingRight, B_CeilingLeft, C_TopBackPanel, D_BottomBackPanel, E_Tabletop, F_TableBase, G_Pitcher, H_Flowers

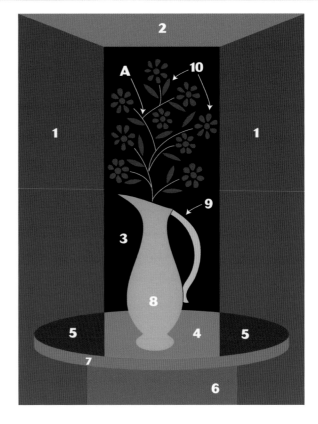

Fuse-by-Number Fabric Reference Chart

	Fabric Description	Size Needed
1	Purple Pebbles	approx. 27" × 33"
2	Green Rolling Squares	19" × 6½"
3	Black Seed Pearls	8½" × 17"
4	Green Rolling Squares	4" × 8"
5	Crimson Grillwork	10" × 3½"
6	Green Holepunch	6½" × 11"
7	Coral Rolling Squares	17" × 8"
8	Orange Blossoms	11" × 11" (5½" × 11")*
9	Green Grass	2" × 6½"
10	Coral Rolling Squares	included with Fabric 7
A	iron-on embellishing thread	one spool or card

fabric needs to be used double-layered to create opacity, avoiding visual bleed-through

Choosing Fabric

Some of the fabrics used here that Yolanda designed are still available; contact us (see page 127) and we can help you find them. However, you can use any fabrics you like. When choosing yours, keep these things in mind:

1 To create the illusion of depth, make Fabric 3 the darkest tone in your fabric range.

2 Making Fabric 8 the brightest tone helps bring the vase forward, creating visual depth. This will require that the fabric for the body of the vase be double-layered so there will be no visual bleed-through from the dark background fabric. The slightly thicker vase will further enhance the sense of dimension. A fabric with a circular texture emphasizes the shape of the vase.

3 Having fabrics 5 and 7 related in hue adds dimension as well. Fabric 5, which was used for the table edge and the flowers, is fairly bright to bring both the blossoms and the table edge forward.

4 When choosing Fabric 6, a stripe used vertically will ground the whole image and help create the illusion of a table base.

5 A pattern with a pebbly texture was chosen for Fabric 1 to suggest the kind of wall the background might be. A tonal damask could have been chosen for a wallpapered look.

Cut the Fabrics

1 Once you have chosen your fabrics, print out all the templates. The images are already reversed so you can trace them onto the fusible web.

2 Tape the templates together as shown.

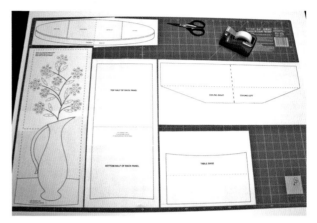

Templates printed and taped.

3 Trace the pieces onto the paper side of the SAS2 that does not peel off as easily. Include the letters and numbers when tracing to match up the letters and numbers later for accurate positioning.

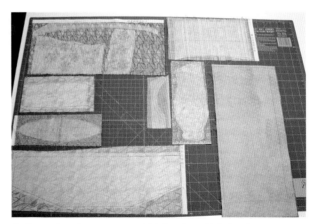

Refer to the chart on page 102 for size of fabric pieces.

Measure and Wrap the Canvas in Fabric

1 It is essential to use a soft tape measure. A tape measure, unlike a stiff ruler, wraps around a canvas the same way fabric would. Refer to the photos to see how to measure the width and height of the canvas. Start at the inner edge of the stretcher frame, go around the front of the canvas and come back around to the back to the opposite inner edge. Measure the length the same way. Based on these measurements, a piece of fabric 32" × 26" is required. Add an inch to both dimensions and cut the fabric to 33" × 27".

The width measures 26".

The height measures 32".

2 Take Fabric 1. You will need to use several pieces of SAS2 to cover the back of the fabric (see diagram). Peel off the loose-paper side and position on the wrong side of the fabric.

26"

32"

| 18" X 32" | 8" X 14" |
| | 8" X 18" |

Piecing together SAS2 for the back.

3 Trim your fused fabric piece down to 32" × 26" and remove, but keep the paper. Cut four 8" × 4" pieces from it. You will use these to help center the canvas on the fabric.

Trimming the fused fabric.

Wrapping Canvas

Once you know how to measure and wrap a canvas in fabric, you can make your own self-framed fusible works of art or a keepsake canvas in any size you like.

4 Lay out the fabric on a large, flat surface, fusible side up. Position the four pieces around the edges of the fabric as shown. Carefully lower the canvas and center on the fabric.

The canvas centered on the fabric.

5 Pat the back of the canvas so the fabric sticks a bit to it. Carefully turn it over so now the fabric is on the top.

The canvas draped in fabric.

6 Pat down the fabric smoothly and evenly so that it adheres to the front of the canvas. Lift up the "skirt" to allow you to pick up your canvas and carry over to your pressing surface.

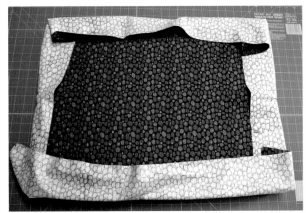

The "skirt" lifted.

7 Let down the "skirt." Make sure all is smooth. Fuse down the fabric with a pressing sheet, working in a circular direction from the center outward. Press down—do not glide—when fusing.

Press, rather than glide, the iron over the fabric.

105

8 Turn up both edges of the shorter side of the canvas and iron down to the back edge of the canvas as shown.

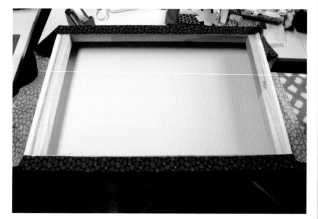

Ironing down the edges.

9 Take each corner and fold as shown.

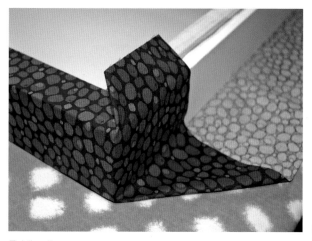

Folding the corners.

Pressing the corners.

10 The canvas will look on both long sides like the picture below.

How the edges look when halfway finished.

11 Fold up the long sides of the fabric.

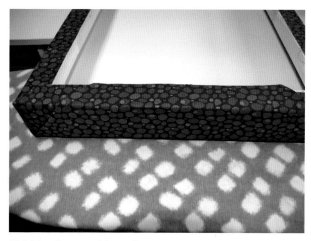

Finishing the remaining edges.

Your corners should look neat and streamlined.

Begin Assembling the Picture

1 Start to build the picture on it from the top of the image.

2 Trace pattern pieces on the paper side of the SAS2 that does not peel off as easily. Peel off the looser paper and fuse the patterns to the wrong side of the fabrics.

3 Cut out Fabric 2 and peel off the second paper backing. Line up the top front edge of the canvas as shown in the first diagram picture. Make sure that it's straight along the front edge of the canvas. *The rest of the picture's alignment depends on this.*

4 Fuse the front down first, then the top edge toward the back. Place on the floor to iron the top edge.

5 Take the shape cut from Fabric 3; peel off the backing, and line it up below Fabric 2. Check that it's straight.

6 Take the shape cut from Fabric 4 and place it below Fabric 2. Fuse both down.

7 Continue cutting out and fusing the pieces in the order shown in the diagrams. You will have to iron the bottom edge similar to the top piece.

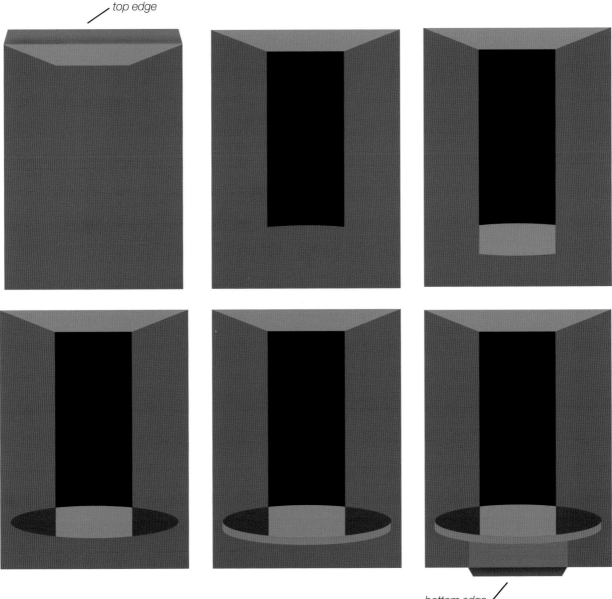

top edge

bottom edge

Place the Pitcher and Flowers

1 For the body of the pitcher, fuse two pieces of Fabric 8 together, right side to wrong side, to create a more opaque piece of fabric. Apply an additional piece of SAS2 to the back of this layered piece with the pitcher shape traced on it, then cut it out. The handle (Fabric 9) doesn't need to be double-layered. Set this aside.

2 Make a tracing of the pitcher and flowers on tracing paper. The template printouts are reversed, so you turn your tracing over. Include the letters and numbers so you can match them to the fusible-backed fabric pieces. Tape the tracing paper to the canvas. Masking tape or blue painter's tape works well for this.

3 Transfer the outlines of the pieces a transfer medium such as Clover Chacopy transfer paper. Though Clover warns of the dangers of setting your chalk lines into the fabric when using an iron, our experience has been that the chalk lines fade quite a bit when used with the Bo-nash Non-Stick Ironing & Craft Sheet. You might want to test the performance of your particular products on a scrap of fabric. Once you have transferred the image to the canvas, fuse down the pitcher and handle and then proceed with all the leaves and flowers. Flip the tracing up and out of the way to position the pieces and then down to check and adjust the placement. Do not remove the tracing yet.

Tracing paper guide for placement.

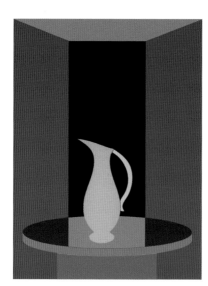
The vase added.

The flowers added.

Apply Fusible Thread

1 At this point, because the tracing lines might have faded during the fusing process, you might need to refresh the tracing of the stems.

2 Pre-heat the mini-iron at its highest setting for about two minutes. The fusible threads require a really hot iron to fuse permanently.

3 If you don't have adhesive Teflon already protecting the mini-iron tip (highly recommended if you are going to be doing a lot of thread fusing), then use a small piece of Teflon pressing sheet between the iron and the fusible thread and fabric. (Refer to pages 66–71 for a refresher on applying fusible thread.)

4 Decide which of the traced stems are the main branches and which are secondary (coming off a main branch). Fuse all the secondary branches first and then apply the main branches. By doing this, the ends of the secondary branches will be covered with the main branch threads.

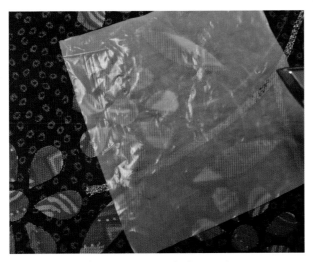

A Teflon pressing sheet between the iron and thread during fusing.

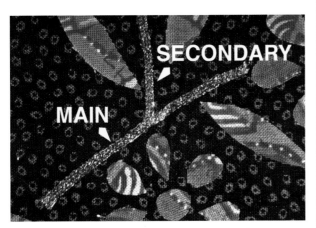

Fuse secondary branches first so the main branch can be positioned to hide the ends.

You have your first fuse-by-number masterpiece ready to hang!

Paper Dolls and Fabric Fashions

Doll height: 11"

What little girl young or old wouldn't have great fun making clothes for paper dolls? And future fashion designers take note: As a young man, Yves St. Laurent was photographed playing with paper dolls to try out his garment ideas. The thought of using actual fabrics to make the clothes excited Yolanda so much that she had to draw up some dolls to play with also. Barbara, who tends to express herself in a much more seemingly manner, shamelessly used her granddaughter and her friend as an excuse for playing with the dolls.

Materials

▶ **Fusing Supplies:**

1 piece Floriani Heat N Sta Fusible Light Fleece®, least 4" × 9"

Steam-A-Seam 2 fusible web: (3) 8½" × 11" pieces for dolls, smaller pieces as needed for clothing

Fusible Velcro

¼" Steam-A-Seam 2 fusible tape

June Tailor Quick Fuse fabric sheets, or regular printable fabric sheets (optional)

Suggested embellishments for decorating clothes: Clover Quick Bias fusible tape, Hot Ribbon Art, fusible threads and crystals

▶ **Other Materials:**

Slightly heavy paper stock (we used Epson Ultra Premium Presentation Paper Matte)

8½" × 11" paper (thinner)

Fabric scraps

▶ **Tools and Templates:**

Inkjet printer (with color ink)

Iron

Teflon pressing sheet

Small, sharp scissors

Fabric marker (erasable)

Artwork and templates from the CD: Aleesha, Lily, Sarah, Clothes1–3, ClothesA, ClothesB

Make the Paper Dolls

1 Print out the paper doll templates using good-quality, slightly heavy paper and the best-quality setting on your printer.

2 Peel off the looser of the two protective papers from an 8½" × 11" piece of SAS2.

3 Hand-press the SAS2 on the back of the doll printout. Then carefully peel off the second protective paper. Place a thinner piece of 8½" × 11" paper on the now-exposed fusible web. Fuse the printout onto the thinner paper by pressing with an iron over a pressing sheet. This additional piece of paper will give the doll better stability.

With an adult's help, kids can try this project. Caitlyn (at right) tended toward fancy dress designs. Her best friend Daniella (below) made pants and T-shirts for her dolls because that's how she likes to dress.

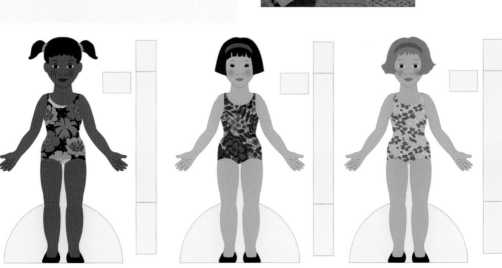

4 Cut out the doll and its two stand pieces with small, sharp scissors. If you are supervising a child they might need help with this, especially with cutting the area around the hands.

5 Make a template out of paper or thin cardboard by transferring onto it the bathing suit shape on one of the dolls. Or, you can print out one more paper doll and cut out the bathing suit to make a bathing-suit-shaped hole.

A cut-out bathing suit template.

6 Trace the bathing suit shape onto the piece of fusible fleece three times.

Tracing the bathing suit on the fusible fleece.

7 Cut along the drawn line and fuse the fleece to the paper doll. The rougher, more textured, shiny side of the fleece is the fusible side. Make sure to use the pressing sheet as you iron. The fleece will provide the base for the Velcro hooks you will be attaching to the dolls' clothes.

The fleece bathing suit placed.

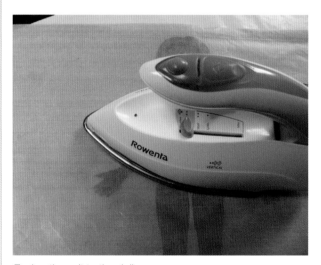

Fusing the suit to the doll.

Kids Can Fuse, Too

Children ages 8 and up can help with this project, as long as they have close, constant adult supervision when handling the iron to fuse. However, we do NOT recommend letting kids under 12 handle crystal applicator tools under any circumstances. If you're uncomfortable with any hot-tool handling, let the kids assist in other ways: designing outfits, cutting out the clothes, etc.

Make the Dolls Stand Up

1 Fold the longer yellow rectangle as shown.

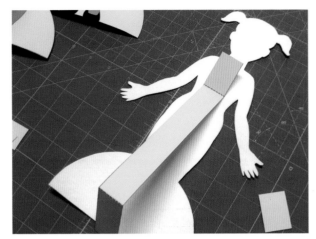

How the main supporting rectangle should fold.

2 Attach it with tape to the base as shown, forming a hinge.

The main rectangle support taped to the base.

3 Tape the smaller yellow rectangle across the top and the sides as shown. This forms a pocket that you can tuck the longer piece into, so you are forming an easel back to stand up the doll. You can untuck the piece and flatten it out again when putting away your doll.

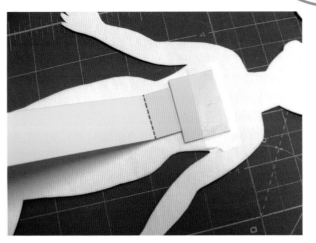

The main supporting rectangle tucked into the pocket.

Create the Clothes

There are three template sheets to help you make your own clothes: Clothes1, Clothes2 and Clothes3.

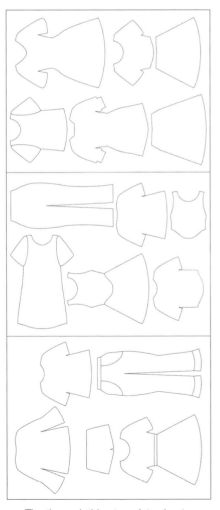

The three clothing template sheets.

1 Print the clothes template sheets onto the same heavier paper stock used for the dolls. Loosely cut out the clothing shapes and use SAS2 or another lightweight fusible web to fuse the wrong side of the pattern to the wrong side of your selected fabric.

Fusible web on the wrong side of fabric.

Printout on top of fusible web on the wrong side of fabric.

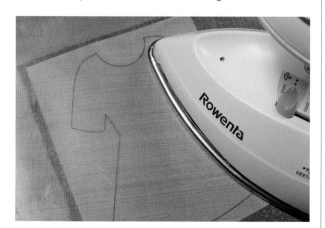

Printout, fusible web and fabric are fused together.

2 Cut out the dress using the outline on the paper side as a guide. Attach a piece of fusible Velcro (use the side with the hooks only) to the paper side of all your custom-made clothing. The Velcro hangs on to the fusible fleece nicely.

3 Embellish the clothes with other fusibles as desired. Refer to teaching projects earlier in the book for specific hints and instructions on how to apply embellishments.

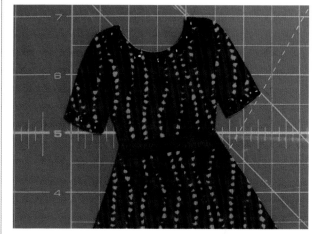

A red dress embellished with Clover Quick Bias fusible tape and Kreinik fusible crystals.

A blouse to which we fused a felt decoration found in the scrapbooking section of our local craft store. We used a small piece of fusible web to attach the flower.

Pants made from the fabric of discarded jeans, with embroidered ribbon fused to the cuffs using SAS2 tape.

Lily models the fancy red party dress, while Aleesha wears a summer play outfit.

On the included CD are also two sheets of preprinted clothes that you can print onto either regular printable fabric or June Tailor Quick Fuse fabric sheets. Then use the same techniques just described for making the doll clothes.

A Place to Call Home

Walnut Hollow makes a nice hinged, unfinished wood cornice box (#3213) that measures 3.36" × 11.96" × 9.19" (see "Resources" on page 126). The dolls fit perfectly in it, with plenty of room for an expanding wardrobe collection. We decorated ours.

Time for Tea Clock

Finished size: 14" diameter

Whenever we meet for an all-day work session, we always break for tea around 3 P.M. This is a nice time to chat and enjoy each other's company. It's a great way to lessen the stress of deadlines that we are often trying to meet. This fabric-covered wooden clock is a reminder to take the time to relax and smell the ginger tea.

Materials

Fusing Supplies:

1 yd. 18" wide Steam-A-Seam 2 fusible web, recut into 3 pieces: 18" × 18", 10" × 12" and 4" × 4"

(Note: SAS2 comes in both 12" and 18" widths. If using 12", buy additional yardage and piece the 18" square.)

Other Materials:

Walnut Hollow Clock Crafts™ 3-piece kit for ⅜" thick faces (#23850)

Walnut Hollow 14" Gallery Baltic Birch Clock Blank (#27636)

Large tracing paper: (2) 14" × 17" pieces taped together to form (1) 28" × 17" piece, or the equivalent to make a piece at least 17" square

18" square black background fabric

10" × 12" piece red fabric for teapot and (12) ½" squares

4" × 4" piece white-and-red fabric for heart

Tools and Templates:

Inkjet printer

Tracing paper

Transfer paper (Clover Chacopy)

Ballpoint pen

Fabric marker (erasable)

Tape

Iron

Teflon pressing sheet

Craft knife

Small scissors

Rotary cutter and mat

Quilter's grid ruler

Stiff backing board, at least 20" × 20"

Templates from the CD: TeapotTemplate, LowerLeftClock, LowerRightClock, UpperLeftClock, UpperRightClock

Prepare the Clock Face and Appliqué Pieces

1 Trace the wooden clock blank onto the tracing paper.

2 Add approximately 1½" all around to the tracing. We used a spool that happened to be almost that exact height to help us draw this.

Using a spool to draw the outer circle evenly.

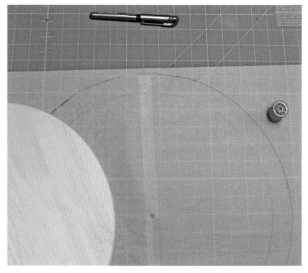

Wooden clock piece and the larger outer circle traced.

3 Draw another circle approximately ½" inside the larger one. Trim the tracing paper to the outer circle.

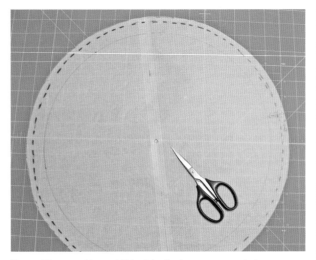

Dotted line marking a ½" inside the larger outer circle.

4 Take the trimmed tracing paper and outline the circle onto the non-loose paper side of the 18" × 18" SAS2 piece (or onto your equivalent piece made up of taped-together smaller pieces.) Make sure you trace *and* tape on the side of SAS2 where the paper is *not* loose.

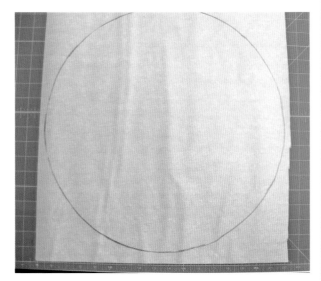

The outer circle traced onto the fusible web.

5 Trim the SAS2 and peel off the looser paper side. Place it on the backing board. Press and fuse it onto the wrong side of your background fabric square.

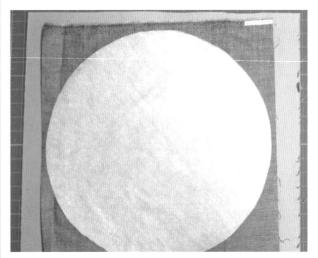

The fusible-web circle fused onto the wrong side of the background fabric.

6 Once fused, trim off excess fabric.

Trimming away the excess background fabric.

7 Center the wooden clock blank face down on the background fabric. Turn over and smooth the fabric down on the face. Turn it over again so it's lying face down.

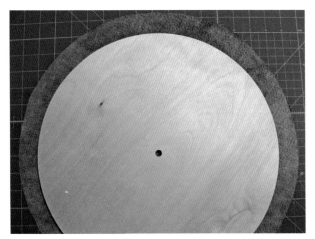

The wooden clock blank on the background fabric.

8 Snip all around the circle every ¾" or so, cutting almost to the clock edge.

Snipping the fabric around the circle.

9 Place the clock back on the board and fold over and fuse down the fabric tabs all around.

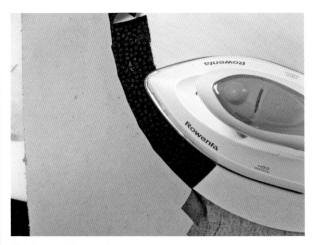

Folding and fusing down the tabs.

10 Turn the clock over and fuse down the fabric on the front.

11 Print out the "TeapotTemplate" file from the CD.

12 Trace the outline onto the harder-to-remove paper side of the SAS2. Position the tracing so you can also cut out at least twelve ½" squares from the same piece. You might want to also sketch these out on the paper backing. Fuse the SAS2 to the wrong side of the 10" × 12" piece of red fabric.

13 Trace the heart in the same fashion on the 4" × 4" piece of SAS2, and fuse to the wrong side of the 4" × 4" white-and-red fabric.

14 Cut out all pieces without removing the protective paper backing, and set aside.

Assemble the Fabric Pieces

1 Print out the four other clock template files, and tape them together as shown.

The four partial clock templates taped together.

2 Place the round tracing paper piece on top of it and trace all the elements onto it.

Copying the design onto tracing paper.

3 Flip over the tracing and center it as accurately as possible on the face of the clock.

The traced guide, flipped appropriately.

4 Transfer the design to the clock face using your transfer paper and a ballpoint pen. We find it best to trace along the inside curve of the marked lines.

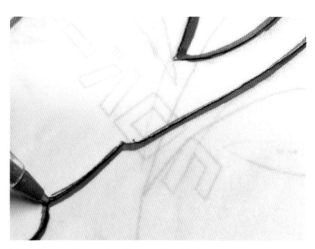

Transferring the design lines to the fabric.

Remember to flip tracing over so it looks like the photo of the finished clock, or this could happen!

5 Carefully fuse down all the pieces, using your transferred lines and tracing as a guide.

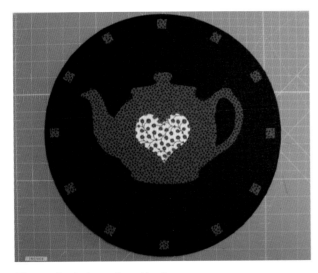

The appliqué pieces fused in place.

Assemble the Clock Parts

1 Feel for the center hole on the clock face and carefully, with a very sharp craft knife, cut through the three layers of fabric and fusible web. Make another cut perpendicular to the first one.

Making the center cut.

2 Open the clock kit and carefully lay out the parts checking, with the diagram on the package to learn what the parts are.

3 Position the rubber cushion over the shaft as explained on the packaging and push through the hole from the back of the clock, to check if you need to cut the fabric open a bit more.

Checking the size of the center fabric opening.

4 Remove the excess fabric by snipping pieces off carefully.

5 Push the shaft through again and trim the fabric carefully with a sharp craft knife or sharp scissors until you have made the opening as flush as possible to the clock face.

Trimming excess fabric from the center hole.

Cleaning up the fabric around the shaft.

6 Once satisfied with the opening, assemble the clock parts as instructed by the packaging. You will need to leave out the piece mentioned in step 4, the dial plate washer. The fabric that is fused to the clock face will act in the same capacity as this part.

7 Align the clock mechanism with the clock face properly, find a battery and hang your clock.

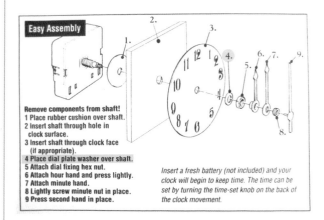

Easy Assembly

Remove components from shaft!
1 Place rubber cushion over shaft.
2 Insert shaft through hole in clock surface.
3 Insert shaft through clock face (if appropriate).
4 Place dial plate washer over shaft.
5 Attach dial fixing hex nut.
6 Attach hour hand and press lightly.
7 Attach minute hand.
8 Lightly screw minute nut in place.
9 Press second hand in place.

Insert a fresh battery (not included) and your clock will begin to keep time. The time can be set by turning the time-set knob on the back of the clock movement.

Skip step 4 of the clock assembly instructions, which mentions a part you won't need for this particular clock.

Tea cozy, side 1

Tea cozy, side 2

Make a matching tea cozy by adapting the instructions for the cozy on page 37. Use the same teapot pattern to create place mats or a table topper for a lovely coordinated kitchen set.

Idea Sparkers: Artist Trading Cards

ATCs are essentially the no-sew counterparts of fabric postcards. Fine artists, fiber artists, scrapbookers, crafters, quilters and all those in between share creative possibilities by exchanging them with each other. Their size makes them an appealing format to test out techniques and explore ideas. And better yet, it lets you send these "idea seeds" in an easy format to others in your creative circle. All in all, it's a great way to begin exploring the wide and wonderful world of fusing.

Here's a sampling of the cards made as part of the Art2Mail™ project (to find out more, visit www.art2mail.com).

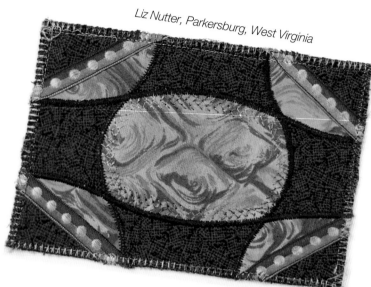

Liz Nutter, Parkersburg, West Virginia

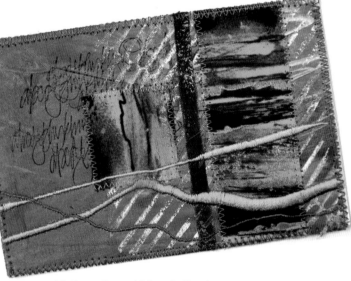

Liz Berg, Castro Valley, California

Susan Wolf Swartz, Highland Park, Illinois

Sue Kelly, St. Cloud, Minnesota

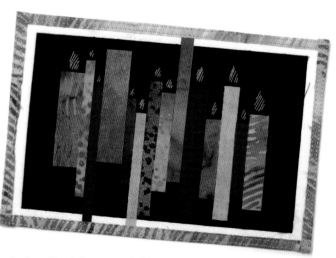

Darlene Steel, Portsmouth, New Hampshire

Fusing has countless benefits, so make it a regular part of your creative process.
As these artists have shown, there are no limits to how it can enhance your projects.

"Heather" by quilt artist Bonnie McCaffery from Milford, Pennsylvania. (www.bonniemccaffery.com)

Finished size: 10½" × 13½"

Lorelei detail of a large bed quilt made by Karen Anderson of Blairstown, New Jersey.

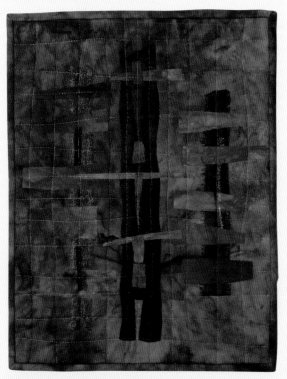

"Black Hills Gold' journal quilt made by fiber artist and quiltmaker Linda Salitrynski from Rome, Pennsylvania. (countrykeepsakesonline.com)

Finished size: 9" × 7"

"Sunday Morning," made by award-winning quiltmaker Esterita Austin, who developed Misty Fuse. (www.esteritaaustin.com)

Finished size: 54" × 59"

Resources

Fusible Products and Tools

There are many manufacturers of fusible (and non-fusible) products who helped to make this book possible. Here is a list of the companies we've worked with, who manufacture and distribute some of the products mentioned in the book.

Textura Trading Company
(Angelina Fiber)
Eastworks Building
116 Pleasant St., Suite 343
Easthampton, MA 01027
(877) 839-8872
www.texturatrading.com

Bo-Nash
P.O. Box 1797
Auburn, WA 98071
(800) 527-8811
www.bonash.com

Clover Needlecraft, Inc.
13438 Alondra Blvd.
Cerritos, CA 90703-2315
(800) 233-1703
www.clover-usa.com

Floriani Embroidery, Sewing &
Quilting Products
RNK Distributing
3400 Division St.
Knoxville, TN 37919
(877) 331-0034
www.rnkdistributing.com

Hot Ribbon Art
Imagination International, Inc.
P.O. Box 928
Eugene, OR 97440
(541) 684-0013
www.hotribbon.com

J.T. Trading Corp.
(Spray and Fix products)
458 Danbury Rd., Unit A18
New Milford, CT 06776
(860) 350-5565
www.jttrading.com
www.sprayandfix.com

June Tailor
P.O. Box 208
2861 Highway 175
Richfield, WI 53076
(800) 844-5400
www.junetailor.com

Kandi Corp.
P.O. Box 8345
Clearwater, FL 33758
(800) 985-2634
www.kandicorp.com

Kreinik Manufacturing Co., Inc.
1708 Gihon Rd.
Parkersburg, WV 26102
(800) 537-2166
www.kreinik.com

Mistyfuse
www.mistyfuse.com

Pellon
4720-A Stone Dr.
Tucker, GA 30084
(800) 223-5275
www.pellonideas.com

Sten Source® International, Inc.
(laser-cut fusible appliqués)
18971 Hess Ave.
Sonora, CA 95370
(800) 642-9293
www.stensource.com

Sullivans USA
4341 Middaugh Ave.
Downers Grove, IL 60515
(800) 862-8586
www.sullivans.net/usa

Superior Threads
87 East 2580 South
St. George, UT 84790
(800) 499-1777
www.superiorthreads.com

Therm O Web
770 Glenn Ave.
Wheeling, IL 60090
(847) 520-5200
www.thermoweb.com

Walnut Hollow Farm, Inc.
1409 State Road 23
Dodgeville, WI 53533
(800) 950-5101
www.walnuthollow.com

The Warm Company
5529 186th Place SW
Lynnwood, WA 98037
(425) 248-2424
www.warmcompany.com

Other Products and Resources

Included in this list are some non-fusible products that are specific to projects in this book.

Bold Over Batiks!
(handmade fabric)
458 Warwick St.
St. Paul, MN 55105
(888) 830-7455
www.boldoverbatiks.com

Clotilde, LLC (Perfect Pleater)
P.O. Box 7500
Big Sandy, TX 75755-7500
(800) 545-4002
www.clotilde.com

Hollander's
(book binder's board)
410 N. Fourth Ave.
Ann Arbor, MI 48104
(734) 741-7531
www.hollanders.com

Miracle Chalk (Chubby Crayon)
540 O'Farrell Ave. SE
Olympia, WA 98501
(360) 357-7858
www.miraclechalk.com

Love in Stitches (Home of the Jersey Girls)
P.O. Box 257
Pine Brook, NJ 07058
www.loveinstitches.com

Visit Barbara and Yolanda's website to order fabrics, patterns, kits and books. Also on the website, see a quilt gallery, download free patterns, get basic quilting instructions and learn more about this creative partnership.

Contributors

It is with much thanks that we feature some of our friends who helped with creating or inspiring projects for this book.

Nina designed and made the no-sew belt and headband on page 98.

Nina Kolpin

After graduating from the Fashion Institute of Technology, Nina worked as a designer for a fine jewelry company in New York. Using her design background, she transitioned into product development. Her background also includes positions within the gift industry, further broadening her creativity. She is currently working for Northcott/Monarch and learning business development for the quilting and fabric industry.

Marta provided the inspiration piece and her templates for the tea cozy on page 37.

Marta McDowell

Marta lives, gardens, writes and stitches in Chatham, New Jersey. Her book *Emily Dickinson's Gardens* was published in 2004. She teaches landscape history at the New York Botanical Garden. She and Yolanda are collaborating on a fine art/gardening book and the traveling exhibit "A Garden Alphabetized."

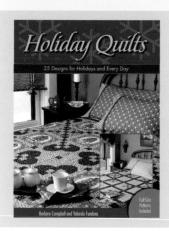

More from Barbara and Yolanda...

Holiday Quilts
25 Designs for Holidays and Every Day
by Barbara Campbell & Yolanda Fundora

Double your quilting pleasure with this one-of-a-kind quilt book, with step-by-step instructions for creating 10+ holiday themed quilts and home décor items, including a tree skirt and table centerpiece.

Paperback • 128 p • 225 color photos
Item# Z0746 • ISBN 13: 978-0-89689-482-2 • ISBN 10: 0-89689-482-7

... plus more fast, easy sewing ideas

Low-Sew Boutique
25 Quick & Clever Projects Using Ready-Mades
by Cheryl Weiderspahn

Transform common place-mats, towels, potholders and rugs into 25+ innovative fashion accessories, such as a backpack, eyeglass case, and purse by following the detailed instructions and illustrations in this unique guide.

Paperback • 128 p • 175 color photos • **Item# Z0378**
ISBN 13: 978-0-89689-434-1 • ISBN 10: 0-89689-434-7

Rainy Day Applique
Quick & Easy Fusible Quilts
by Ursula Michael

Whatever your sewing skill level, you'll enjoy the time and money saving tips you find in this project-packed guide. Check out the bonus CD with 100+ innovative patterns.

Paperback • 128 p
50 b&w photos • 200 color photos • **Item# Z0936**
ISBN 13: 978-0-89689-539-3 • ISBN 10: 0-89689-539-4

No Sew, Low Sew Decorative Storage
50 Stylish Projects to Stash Your Stuff
by Carol Zentgraf & Elizabeth Dubicki

This collection of 50 inexpensive and easy-to-make storage solutions for the home can be completed with a hot glue gun, basic hand stitches, and other fast and easy techniques. Includes step-by-step instructions and 200 photos.

Paperback • 144 p • 100+ color photos, 50 illus.
Item# DECST • ISBN 13: 978-0-87349-889-0
ISBN 10: 0-87349-889-5

Sew Pretty Homestyle
Over 35 Irresistible Projects to Fall in Love With
by Tone Finnanger

A subtle color palette and lovable designs combine to create a fresh and fun collection of over 35 projects.

Paperback • 144 p • 140 color photos • 100 color illus.
Item# Z1703 • ISBN 13: 978-0-7153-2749-4
ISBN 10: 0-7153-2749-6